I0814607

Saint Joseph

Saint Joseph

THE MAN CLOSEST TO CHRIST

Fr. Sebastian Walshe, O. PRAEM.

TAN Books
Gastonia, North Carolina

Saint Joseph: The Man Closest to Christ © 2023 Norbertine Fathers of Orange, Inc

All rights reserved. With the exception of short excerpts used in critical review, no part of this work may be reproduced, transmitted, or stored in any form whatsoever, without the prior written permission of the publisher. Creation, exploitation and distribution of any unauthorized editions of this work, in any format in existence now or in the future—including but not limited to text, audio, and video—is prohibited without the prior written permission of the publisher.

Unless otherwise noted, Scripture quotations are from the Revised Standard Version of the Bible—Second Catholic Edition (Ignatius Edition), copyright © 2006 National Council of the Churches of Christ in the United States of America. Used by permission. All rights reserved.

Scripture quotations marked (NABRE) are taken from the *New American Bible, Revised Edition* © 2010, 1991, 1986, 1970 Confraternity of Christian Doctrine, Washington, D.C. and are used by permission of the copyright owner. All Rights Reserved. No part of the New American Bible may be reproduced in any form without permission in writing from the copyright owner.

Excerpts from the English translation of the *Catechism of the Catholic Church* for use in the United States of America copyright © 1994, United States Catholic Conference, Inc.—Libreria Editrice Vaticana. Used with Permission.

Cover design by David Ferris—www.davidferrisdesign.com.

Cover image: Saint Joseph and the Christ Child, by Bartolomé Eseteban Murillo. Oil on canvas, ca. 1670-75 / Commons.wikimedia.org.

Library of Congress Control Number: 2022946379
ISBN: 978-1-5051-2727-0
Kindle ISBN: 978-1-5051-2728-7
ePUB ISBN: 978-1-5051-2729-4

Published in the United States by
TAN Books
PO Box 269
Gastonia, NC 28053
www.TANBooks.com

Printed in India

"But as Joseph has been united to the Blessed Virgin by the ties of marriage, it may not be doubted that he approached nearer than any to the eminent dignity by which the Mother of God surpasses so nobly all created natures."

—Pope Leo XIII, *Quamquam Pluries*, no. 3

Contents

Introduction

As the year 2020 was ending, Pope Francis unexpectedly dedicated the following year in honor of Saint Joseph. Perhaps His Holiness sensed that the Church needed a father's special care during the pandemic's difficult times. Many of the faithful, who experience a childlike trust in Saint Joseph, rejoiced greatly in this gift to the whole Church. Among the many fruits of this grace was a deeper emphasis and reflection upon the person of Saint Joseph. This book is one of those many fruits.

While there are many excellent devotional books on Saint Joseph, as well as many private revelations about his life, my intention is to draw primarily from Sacred Scripture and Sacred Tradition. The reason for this is that the fonts of revelation are the very word of God by which all truth is measured; moreover, as the word of God, they contain more powerful seeds of truth which make for a more profound and certain development of doctrine.

However, in writing a book on Saint Joseph based primarily upon Sacred Scripture, the author is immediately confronted with a serious difficulty: Scripture records not even a single word of Saint Joseph.[1] What is there to say about a

[1] It seems to me that there is a mystical significance to the fact that Saint Joseph uttered no word in Scripture: just as Saint Joseph spoke no word in Scripture, so also he did not beget the Word of God. For Jesus

man who said nothing? Our problem is further compounded when we seek to know something about his heavenly glory. Indeed, Saint Joseph's earthly and heavenly life remain very much a mystery. The Scriptures have not even left us a single word uttered by him: not so much as a scrap from the master's table. If we do not know how to speak of earthly things, therefore, how shall we speak of heavenly ones?[2] A man's words are a privileged source of insight into his mind and heart. Absent this source, we would seem to be at a great disadvantage in our attempt to understand Saint Joseph in any meaningful way. Perhaps this is why so many turn to private revelations concerning his life.

Yet Saint Joseph—a man so important in the economy of grace and salvation—cannot be simply ignored by revelation. Where Scripture closes one door, it often opens another. And so we trust in the words of the Lord: "The kingdom of heaven is like a grain of mustard seed which a man took and sowed in his field; it is the smallest of all seeds, but when it has grown it is the greatest of shrubs and becomes a tree, so that the birds of the air come and make nests in its branches" (Mt 13:31). Sacred Scripture has certain passages which are like the smallest seeds and yet filled with the greatest power. Their power is hidden at first, but later, they grow, and the truth they contain extends broader and higher.

In God's providence, it seems that the significance of Saint Joseph should remain largely hidden until the later ages of

---

is the Word begotten by the Father; therefore, the fact that Joseph had no word is a sign meant to indicate that Jesus was not naturally begotten from Joseph.

[2] Cf. Jn 3:12.

the Church. Pope Pius XI once said, "Between these two missions [the missions of Saint John the Baptist and Saint Peter] there appears that of Saint Joseph, one of recollection and silence, one almost unnoticed and destined to be lit up only many centuries afterwards, a silence which would become a resounding hymn of glory, but only after many years."[3] Therefore, these truths—like a buried treasure—are gradually uncovered, allowing the Church to enter more fully into the mystery of Saint Joseph.

Where then should we look in Scripture to understand the interior life of Saint Joseph and the unique role he plays in the economy of grace and salvation? Scripture reminds us that certain personages in the Old Testament are a type, or prefigurement,[4] of those in the New Testament. To cite just a few examples, Adam was a type of Christ (see Rom 5:14) and Elijah was a prefigurement of John the Baptist (see Mt 17:12–13; Lk 1:17). Jonah was a prophetic type of Jesus (see Mt 12:40). Often, the person who prefigures someone in the New Testament can give a clearer indication about some reality or truth about the New Testament personage. For example, the universal influence of Adam over all men sheds light upon the universal influence of Christ over all men (see Rom 5:12–21). And Queen Esther's intercessory role in saving her people prefigures the Blessed Virgin Mary as the

---

[3] Conference delivered on March 19, 1928.

[4] I am using the words "type" and "prefigurement" as synonymous in this book. There are some who would give a refined definition of these terms which distinguishes them from one another. For example, some say that a type must be a historical fact or individual, while a prefigurement need not be.

queen of heaven and earth. This method of explaining Scripture was used copiously by the Fathers of the Church and has been approved by the Church as a legitimate method of understanding revelation.[5]

This book will examine the Old Testament figures who were clear types of Saint Joseph and will argue from the things said about the type to truths about Saint Joseph.[6] But because arguments from typology and the spiritual sense of a passage can only be probable and not the foundations of a certain, theological argument, whenever possible, I will also provide a properly theological argument from the literal sense of Scripture for the same conclusion. Finally, I will provide confirmation of these conclusions from the liturgy or Tradition of the Church. The advantage of arguing first from typology is that types often more clearly and quickly lead to a conclusion which is more obscure and lengthy when reached by a rigorously theological argument. Besides, in those matters for which a rigorous theological argument has not yet been found, arguments from typology at least afford some probable knowledge and can be a great assistance to the devotion of the faithful.

With these principles in mind, let us now turn to the person of Saint Joseph.

---

5 See, for example, *CCC* 128–30; and Leo XIII, *Quamquam Pluries*.

6 Granted that there are many objections which someone might raise against this method as a valid theological method, but I will defend this methodology in greater detail (chapter 2).

Chapter 1

Devotion to Saint Joseph

Understanding Saint Joseph and his place in the economy of grace and salvation is critical for every follower of Jesus. Those who love Jesus also love the things and the people He loved most, especially His heavenly Father and His parents: Joseph and Mary. This investigation is both motivated by devotion to Saint Joseph and meant to increase our devotion to Saint Joseph. Therefore, it is appropriate here to explain why devotion to Saint Joseph is both beneficial and praiseworthy.

The purpose of devotion to Saint Joseph, as with devotion to Mary, is to draw us closer to Jesus. The Scriptures imply that devotion to Joseph increases our love and knowledge of Jesus, for it is there that we find that disdain for Saint Joseph leads to disdain for Jesus:

> The Jews murmured about him because he said, "I am the bread that came down from heaven;" and they said, "Is this not Jesus, the son of Joseph? Do we not know his father and mother? Then how can he say, 'I have come down from heaven'?" (Jn 6:41–42 NABRE)

> He came to his native place and taught the people in their synagogue. They were astonished and said, "Where did this man get such wisdom and mighty deeds? Is he not the carpenter's son? Is not his mother named Mary and his brothers James, Joseph, Simon, and Judas? Are not his sisters all with us? Where did this man get all this?" And they took offense at him. (Mt 13:54–57 NABRE; cf. Lk 4:22)

Despite evidence that Jesus was a remarkable person with divine attributes, the people refused to glorify and reverence Jesus because they held His parents in little esteem. They thought His parents were ordinary, unexceptional people, and so they could not believe in Jesus. So if it is true, as the Scriptures teach, that lack of devotion and esteem for Joseph leads to disdain for Jesus, the converse is also taught by Scripture: devotion and esteem for Saint Joseph leads to love and esteem of Jesus. And at the same time, the more we love Jesus, the more we honor His parents.

One might reasonably ask: "But why should we approach Jesus through devotion to Joseph? Wouldn't it be better to approach Jesus directly?" After all, the person directly next to someone is closer to him than the person who has someone else standing between them. So it would seem that the person who comes directly to Jesus is closer to Jesus than the person who has Saint Joseph standing between him and Jesus. Yet it seems that it is not always true that having something in between increases the distance between two things. Who sees the star more clearly: the one who looks with the naked eye or the one who uses a telescope? In some way, the eye is brought closer to the star because the telescope was placed between them. So the question is: Can Saint Joseph be a kind of instrument or mediator by which we draw closer to Jesus? This question deserves a careful response.

The Divine Economy

To answer the question about whether or not devotion to Saint Joseph draws us closer to Jesus, we must answer a prior question; namely: Does God normally prefer to communicate truth, grace, and salvation directly or through some created instrument? If God normally prefers to use creatures as His instruments for communicating truth, grace, and salvation, it is reasonable to think that God uses certain saints as privileged instruments to bring about a closer union with Him.

Jesus once said: "He who believes in me will also do the works that I do; and greater works than these will he do" (Jn 14:12). That is a remarkable statement, and it came true. For example, Jesus never healed anyone with His shadow, but Peter did (see Acts 5:15). Jesus never converted three thousand persons in one sermon, but Peter did (see Acts 2:41). Some saints performed more remarkable resurrections than Jesus did. For example, Saint Vincent Ferrer raised a child that had been totally dismembered. Why is it that some saints performed greater miracles than Jesus did? Is it because Jesus could not do this Himself? Clearly not. But for some reason, Jesus wanted to do more through Peter and His other disciples than directly Himself. Here are two reasons why God would choose to do greater works through the instrumentality of His saints than directly.

First, every father has the experience of wanting his children to be as good as they can be. In fact, I know of no father who does not desire that his children be better than himself. God is no exception. He wants to communicate as much good as possible to His children, and He wants them to have and be worthy of as much honor as possible. So God communicates the dignity of being true and real causes of salvation to His children. This makes His creatures more like Himself.

A second and perhaps more profound reason God chooses human instruments to communicate His grace and salvation is to strengthen the bonds of love between men. If God truly uses us as instruments of His grace and salvation, if He uses the person who baptized you to give you the divine life, or the priest who absolved your sins to put you in His grace, or the friend who prayed and obtained the grace for your conversion, or whatever, then we shall have them to thank one day for a good as great as salvation itself. When we are safely in our fatherland one day, God willing, we shall be able to look one another in the eye and say, "Thank you. If it had not been for you, I would not have been saved." And this will increase our love for one another in heaven tremendously. Nor will we love God any less, since we will see clearly that all grace and salvation has its original source in God, even though it came to us through instruments, like the fruit from the vine through the branches. So it's a win-win scenario for God if He uses us as His instruments: we will not love God any less, but we will love one another much more. And isn't this what a father most of all desires for his children: that they love one another as much as possible?

Therefore, any theology that claims that God does not ordinarily prefer to use instruments to cause grace and salvation is incompatible with revelation. Furthermore, a theology that denies that God uses instruments as true causes is really the result of a nominalist philosophy which denies universal or secondary causes. Instead, God wants to encourage us to go to Him through His saints. And to do this, He more quickly and readily answers our prayers and gives us greater gifts if we come to Him through them: "They shall do greater works than I."

Let us now apply this principle to the person of Saint Joseph. Together with the Blessed Virgin Mary, Saint Joseph is one of the preeminent examples of a divinely chosen instrument for doing these greater works. Scripture teaches that when the baby Jesus's life was threatened, God chose to save the baby Jesus through the instrumentality of Saint Joseph. It is obvious that God the Father, or even Jesus Himself, could have simply destroyed the troops of Herod with a mere act of their divine will. But instead, God tells Joseph to flee to Egypt and stay there for a time. This involved great personal sacrifice for Saint Joseph, so why didn't God address the problem with His divine power? The clear answer is that God wanted Saint Joseph to receive the honor of having been a true cause of saving Jesus's life. Not only that, but Jesus Himself now had a reason to be grateful to Saint Joseph. Moreover, all Christians have a reason to be thankful to Saint Joseph since he really did save the baby Jesus. Today,

God wills to save us in a similar way—that is, using Saint Joseph as His instrument. Since Joseph was instrumental in the care of Jesus's physical body, so throughout time God wills him to be an instrument in caring for the mystical body of Christ and drawing Christ's members closer to their head. So there is a special reason Christians should foster devotion to Saint Joseph.

Chapter 2

Typology in Scripture and Theology

Scripture itself tells us that certain persons or things are types of other persons or things (e.g., 1 Pt 3; Rom 5; 1 Cor 10). Moreover, the authors of Scripture argue forcefully to a number of important theological conclusions using typology (e.g., Rom 5:12–21). Finally, the Fathers and Doctors of the Church often used typology to explain the meaning of Scripture or to draw out more profound developments in doctrine. The use of types by the Fathers of the Church was so widespread that one would be hard-pressed to find one Father of the Church who did not use typology in his commentaries or homilies on Scripture. Finally, the universal *Catechism of the Catholic Church* endorses a typological method of reading and explaining Scripture.[7] And so both Sacred Scripture and Sacred Tradition have endorsed typology as a method of coming to understand divine revelation. At the same time, it will be helpful to lay down some principles of typology in order to better prepare for its use in interpreting Scripture regarding the person of Saint Joseph.

[7] See *CCC* 115–19, 128–30.

First, I should give a definition of the word "type." The word "type" derives from the Greek word "typos," which originally meant the image stamped upon a coin. From this, it is evident that essential to the meaning of type is the kind of likeness which allows one thing to represent another. Moreover, the images stamped upon coins were usually of some great personage. So a scriptural type, as I am using the word in this book, is *a person or thing*[8] *in Scripture which can be understood as a clear likeness to some greater person or thing which comes later in Scripture.*[9] As such, a type is *fulfilled* in the greater person or thing. For example, Joshua, who led God's people into the Promised Land, is a type of Christ, the waters of the flood are a type of baptism, and the manna in the desert is a type of the Eucharist. It is not always necessary that if the type is a thing, its fulfillment must also be a thing. Sometimes, a type is a thing, but its fulfillment is a person. For example, the bronze serpent is a type of Christ (Nm 21:9; Jn 3:14) and the Ark of the Covenant is a type of Mary. Conversely, sometimes the type is a person, but its

---

[8] By "thing" here, I mean not only physical substances but also actions and words. I do not intend to address the question of whether the person or thing in Scripture need be a historical person or thing in order to be a type (for example, whether Job needs to be an historical person in order to be a type of Christ). In any case, the persons I will be using as types of Saint Joseph seem to be real, historical figures of the Old Testament.

[9] There may be other valid definitions of a type which are used today in the context of theology, and I do not intend to exclude these other related definitions. With this definition of type, I simply intend to indicate clearly what I mean by type in this book, in a way which corresponds to something really found in Scripture and which also corresponds with how the word is used in ordinary speech among interpreters of Scripture, especially the Fathers of the Church.

fulfillment is a thing, as Rahab was a type of the Church gathered from the Gentiles or Hagar was a type of the covenant of Sinai (Gal 4:24).

Typology, therefore, is *a method of leading the mind of someone who believes in Scripture from a knowledge of the type to a more certain or perfect knowledge of the one in whom the type is fulfilled*. For example, when Saint Paul considers Adam as a type of Christ, he leads the minds of believers from a knowledge of Adam's role as universal cause of condemnation to a more perfect knowledge of Christ's role as universal cause of salvation (cf. Rom 5:12–21).

How can we know that some person or thing is a type? Couldn't anyone point out some likeness between two things and claim that it is a type? For example, someone might say that Esau was a man, therefore he is a type of Christ who also is a man. In other words, isn't it purely subjective and arbitrary whether something is called a type or not? The answer to this is that the likeness between the type and its fulfillment must be obvious or *clear*. A likeness is clear when there are *multiple* and *distinct* parallels between the type and its fulfillment. A likeness is *distinct* when it is uncommon or unique. For example, when two people in Scripture share the same name, this is a distinct likeness, especially when it is an uncommon name. Again, the likeness between Jonah and Christ being enclosed for three days, and then freed, is uncommon and unusual. On the other hand, the likeness between Jonah and Christ insofar as both are men, or both walked about a city, is something common which does little to distinguish one person from another. When the parallel shared by two persons or things in Scripture is unique to the two of them, then this is an especially powerful indication that one is a type of the other. For example, it is unique to Adam and Christ that neither of them had a natural, human father. There must also be *multiple*, distinct parallels in order to certify the likeness as a type. As a rule of thumb, *three distinct parallels* are usually sufficient to establish someone or something as a type.[10] But more than three gives even greater certitude that one is a type and the other its fulfillment.

Determining a clear likeness between two persons or things in Scripture is not unlike determining a resemblance between the faces of two people. If two people have only the same shape head or only the same shape eyes, this usually is not enough for us to say they resemble one another. But when three or more likenesses exist, as when their heads, eyes, and noses all have the same shape, this is usually sufficient to cause us to say there is a resemblance. And if besides these, their chins and ears have the same shape, and they have the same color hair, et cetera, the resemblance becomes so pronounced that it is impossible to see the one without calling to mind or remembering the other. And just as the resemblance between two people is not merely subjective or arbitrary, so also the clear likeness between a type and its fulfillment is not merely subjective or arbitrary. The ability of a type to *call to mind* that of which it is a type is the key element which gives force and power to arguments by way of typology.

---

[10] However, if a likeness is sufficiently distinct or unique, even two likenesses may suffice to give certitude (cf. Gn 41:32).

The Benefits of Reading Scripture Using Typology

The first benefit which comes from reading Scripture typologically is that a type can be understood as a kind of prophecy which strengthens the believer's faith. For example, when we read how Jonah was enclosed within the whale for three days, and then we see that Jesus too was enclosed in the earth for three days, this confirms that Jonah was meant to point to Christ (see Mt 12:40). Or again, when we read how Joshua (which also can be translated "Jesus") was the one who lead the people of Israel into the Promised Land, this has a prophetic meaning concerning Jesus, who shall lead God's people into heaven. These prophetic types strengthen the faith of the believer that Jesus was the risen Savior prefigured by Jonah and Joshua. When we read in Judith that she will "do a thing which will go down through all generations of our descendants" (Jdt 8:32) and that she is "blessed by the Most High God above all women on earth" (Jdt 13:18) because she severed the head of the enemy general, Holofernes, or when we read that Jael is called "most blessed of women" because she fatally wounded the Canaanite general Sisera in the head (Jgs 5:24), these have a prophetic meaning concerning Mary, who would strike a fatal blow to the head of Satan our enemy (cf. Gn 3:15; Lk 1:50; Lk 1:42).

Reading Scripture typologically can also allow us to understand profound theological insights quicker than by means of strict theological demonstrations from the literal sense of Scripture. How does this happen? A type has clear likenesses to that of which it is a type. These clear or open elements of likeness cause the mind to pay closer attention to the type and its fulfillment and to examine in greater detail the relationship which exists between them. Through this reflection, other likenesses between the type and its fulfillment which were at first hidden become more apparent. The open elements of likeness allow us to see clearly that it is a type, while the hidden elements of likeness allow us to come to know the fulfillment of the type more perfectly. The following examples will help illustrate and clarify this point.

First Example: The Exodus as a Type of the Journey of the Soul

The Israelites' journey from Egyptian slavery to the Promised Land is a type of journey for the soul: from sin to heaven. The similarities between both journeys is evident:

1. Pharaoh is like Satan since he, like Satan, is a powerful and cruel tyrant who unjustly holds God's people in utter slavery.
2. Egypt is like a state of sin since in Egypt the people of God are in bondage, prevented from worshiping the Lord, and tempted by the goods of the flesh (see Ex 16:3).
3. The ten plagues of Moses are like the Ten Commandments. For just as the plagues come from Moses, so do the Commandments. And just as there are ten plagues, so there are Ten Commandments. Finally, just as the plagues were painful incentives to allow the Egyptians to let Israel go free, so too the Ten Commandments are a cause of pain of conscience

in the believer's soul which are an incentive to depart from sin.

4. The crossing of the Red Sea is like Baptism (see 1 Cor 10:2). For just as the matter of Baptism is water, so too the Red Sea is water. And just as one who is baptized is immersed into the water, so too the Israelites were within the water as they crossed the Red Sea. Finally, just as Baptism destroys the authority of Satan over the soul, so too when Israel crossed the Red Sea, the authority of Pharaoh was destroyed.
5. The journey across the desert resembles the passage of the Christian soul through this life. As the desert is an intermediate place through which the Israelites were traveling in order to reach their true homeland, so too this life is an intermediate place through which the Christian must travel in order to reach his true homeland. And just as the desert is a place of testing to see if the people were worthy to enter the Promised Land, so too this life is a place of testing to see if the Christian soul is worthy to enter heaven.
6. The manna is like the Eucharist because both have the form of bread with heavenly and miraculous origins. Moreover, just as the manna miraculously apportioned out to be enough for each one who gathered (see Ex 16:17–18), so too the whole Christ is found under the form of bread no matter the size of the bread consumed.
7. The entrance into the Promised Land is like the soul's entrance into heaven. For as the Promised Land was

> the land promised by God as the everlasting heritage of His people (see Dt 4:40), so too heaven is the everlasting heritage of the Christian soul. And just as the Promised Land abounded with delights and peace (see Dt 27:3), so too does heaven.

There are seven distinct likenesses between the Exodus journey and the Christian soul's journey. Truly, the journey of Exodus is a type of the journey of the Christian soul.[11] Once we have seen that the Exodus is a type, we can go back and examine some interesting details of the Exodus. Upon closer inspection, we notice another significant element of the journey from Egypt into the Promised Land: the forty years wandering the desert after turning back at the border of the Promised Land. Now, if the Exodus is a type corresponding to the journey of the Christian soul, then it is probable that this significant element of the Exodus also has a likeness to the journey of the soul from sin to glory. Once we recognize this connection, we see the likeness with even greater clarity: the forty years in the desert is like an intermediate state between this life and the eternal life of heaven, a temporary state where faults are purified. In other words, the forty years in the desert corresponds to the Catholic understanding of purgatory. Note the similarities:

1. Just as the wandering in the desert was a punishment because God's people were not disposed to enter the

[11] In terms of the senses of Scripture, this would be a good example of the moral sense of Scripture in which the events of Scripture are a sign which teaches the believer how he should act in this life.

Promised Land, so too purgatory is a punishment for those who are not disposed to enter heaven.

2. Just as that part of God's people who were not ready to enter the Promised Land all died off during the wandering in the desert, so too those parts of the soul which are not fit for heaven are purified during purgatory.
3. In Scripture, the number forty signifies a time of cleansing or purification (e.g., the forty days and nights of the flood, Moses and Elijah fast for forty days and forty nights in preparation to see God, etc.). So also the forty years in the desert signifies a time of purgation analogous to purgatory.

This type points clearly to the doctrine of purgatory. Notice that the strict theological argument for the existence of purgatory takes some time to work out and was only clearly given expression in the late patristic period.[12] Yet the same conclusion can be reached sooner by means of typology. Sometimes a type will give the reader a clue that some statement is a revealed truth (e.g., the statement that purgatory exists). This clue can then be set down as a provisional goal or conclusion to see if a properly theological argument can be made. Just as one who already knows the conclusion often finds the argument for that conclusion more quickly, so also one who sees some truth by way of typology can often find an appropriate theological argument more quickly. This is like the case when someone who knows the right answer to a

---

[12] See the appendix for a summary of the argument for the existence of purgatory.

math problem often finds the argument more quickly. And if a strict theological demonstration for that truth is found, the fact that there was a type all along confirms the theological argument because evidence for the conclusion is found directly in the text of Scripture.

Second Example: Esther as a Type of Mary

Queen Esther is one of the many holy women of the Old Testament who is a type of Mary, the Mother of Jesus. Here are some notable likenesses between them:

1. Just as Esther was raised up from relative obscurity and a humble state of life to the highest royal dignity, so too the Blessed Virgin Mary was raised up from an obscure and humble station to be the Queen of Heaven.
2. Just as Esther was favored "above all women" by the King (Est 2:17 Vulgate), so was the Blessed Virgin Mary declared "highly favored" by God and "blessed among women" (Lk 1:28 Vulgate).
3. Just as Esther was chosen to take the place of a woman who should have been queen (Queen Vashti), so the Blessed Virgin Mary was chosen in the place of Eve, becoming the new Eve.
4. Just as Esther was an intercessor who saved God's people from the wicked Haman, so too the Blessed Virgin Mary is an intercessor who, by her prayers, obtains salvation for God's people from Satan.
5. Just as Esther, in spite of her fear, had to choose to take a grave risk and enter into the presence of the

> king in order to save God's people, so too the Blessed Virgin Mary, in spite of her fear, had to take a grave risk of becoming the Mother of God in order to save God's people.

So those are five distinct likenesses which show that Esther is a type of the Blessed Virgin Mary. Now let us look at two other elements in the life of Queen Esther as recorded in Scripture. Esther approached King Ahasuerus in the first place because an edict had been promulgated that all of the Jews in the kingdom were to be destroyed. Thus her people stood under a universal condemnation. When Esther wavers at the request of Mordochi, he responds to her: "If you will now hold your peace, the Jews shall be delivered by some other occasion" (Est 4:14 Vulgate). Moreover, there was a universal law, punishable by death, that none should enter the presence of the king without being summoned. To reassure her, King Ahasuerus says to her: "Fear not: you shall not die. For this law is made not for you, but for all others" (Est 15:13 Vulgate). Granted that Esther is a type of the Blessed Virgin Mary, what could these two elements mean?

The first passage could be interpreted to mean that if the Blessed Virgin Mary had refused to accept her mission to be the Mother of God, God would have found another way to save us. This highlights the fact that God's first intention was to save fallen mankind and that the Blessed Virgin Mary was a means to this end. This also indicates how God primarily loves the common good of the elect, as Saint Augustine once wrote: "The Virgin Mary is both holy and blessed, and yet the Church is greater than she. Mary is a part of the Church, a member of the Church, a holy, an eminent—the most eminent—member, but still only a member of the entire body. The body undoubtedly is greater than she, one of its members."[13]

As for the second passage, it seems to refer to Our Lady's special privilege as exempt from the universal law of original sin which has condemned our race to death. In other words, it can be understood to refer to her immaculate conception. So those are two interesting theological conclusions which can be reached with some probability using typology.

Types and Antitypes

One obvious objection to arguing from types as described above is that together with the many likenesses which exist between a type and its fulfillment, there are also many differences. How can someone be certain, therefore, when they are arguing from the type to the fulfillment, that they are actually arguing to another likeness? Maybe what seems like a likeness to one person is in fact a difference. For example, Saint Paul says that Adam is a type of Christ. Therefore, someone might argue thus: Adam is a type of Christ, but Adam sinned, so therefore we can say that Christ also sinned. Or again, Adam is a type of Christ, but Adam took a wife, therefore Christ must have taken a wife. These conclusions are clearly erroneous. And so it seems that arguing from types is an invalid method of deepening our understanding of Scripture and divine revelation.

This objection helps us to refine our understanding about how types can be used in interpreting Scripture and drawing

---

[13] Sermon 25, 7–8: PL 46, 937–38.

theological conclusions therefrom. First of all, just because two things are alike in some respects, it does not follow that they are alike in every respect. It is possible that a type might be unlike its fulfillment in significant ways. Hence, the fact that something is a type does not, by itself, guarantee that we can draw a true conclusion about the thing prefigured in every case. The example of Adam and Christ makes this abundantly clear.

When interpreting Scripture, it is essential to pay attention to the three principles which the *Catechism of the Catholic Church* lays out for interpreting Scripture: (1) Be especially attentive to the content and unity of the whole of Scripture; (2) Read the Scripture within the living Tradition of the Church; and (3) Be attentive to the analogy of faith—that is, to the coherence of the truths of faith among themselves.[14] If we keep these principles in mind, the example of Adam and Christ presents no difficulty. For, other texts in Scripture clearly state that Christ did not sin (e.g., 1 Pt 2:22), and the Tradition of the Church clearly holds that Christ was never married.

If these three principles are observed, we can sometimes discover a revelation even in the differences between a type and its fulfillment. For the very same text might be understood in a spiritual manner so that its application to the fulfillment is apt and consonant with revelation. Take the example of Adam and Christ. Adam sinned, and this cannot be applied to Christ. Yet, in a way, we might say that Christ took upon Himself the whole of Adam's sin in all

[14] See *CCC* 112–14.

of its extension and effects. Thus, Saint Paul could say that "he made him to be sin who knew no sin, so that in him we might become the righteousness of God" (2 Cor 5:21). Or when we note that Adam took a wife to himself, we can also apply this to Christ who took the Church as His bride: "Husbands, love your wives, as Christ loved the church and gave himself up for her to sanctify her, that he might sanctify her, having cleansed her by the washing of water with the word, that he might present the church to himself in splendor, without spot or wrinkle or any such thing, that she might be holy and without blemish" (Eph 5:25–27). It was by this same method that the Fathers of the Church saw that Adam, when God formed Eve from his side while he slept, was a type of the dead Christ on the cross from whose side the Church was formed.

Sometimes the Scriptural types are proposed in such a way that one is an antitype of the other.[15] This can happen in two ways. In the first way, the person or thing is both a type and an antitype: a type in respect to the many likenesses which exist between it and its fulfillment, but an antitype in respect to the differences. In this way, Adam is both a type and antitype of Christ: a type insofar as he is the universal father of mankind, but an antitype insofar as he is the universal father of sin. In a second way, the person or thing is only an

[15] By the word "antitype" here, I do not mean to signify the fulfillment of the type (the way Baptism is called an antitype of the flood, for example, in 1 Pt 3:21). Rather, by the word "antitype," I mean to signify a person or thing which represents in a clear way the opposite of the type. For example, Absalom can be considered an antitype of Christ (see 2 Sm 18) or Hagar can be considered an antitype of the Virgin Mary (see Gn 16:7–12).

antitype, which is shown by the many distinct yet parallel differences between the antitype and that of which it is an antitype. For example, Lucifer is an antitype of Christ insofar as both are a kind of firstborn, but one as creature, the other as creator; both are a kind of universal cause, but one of sin, the other of righteousness; both are kings, but one of the just, the other of the unjust; both sought a condition not natural to them, but one sought to exalt himself above his nature, while the other emptied Himself below His nature.

Looking at the many parallels between something and its antithesis can also reveal deeper insights as well. An interesting case is seen in the persons of King David and King Ahab. The Scriptures draw a clear parallel between David and Ahab. Both were kings of Israel. David took possession of Bathsheba and murdered Uriah, while Ahab murdered Naboth and took possession of his vineyard: "Have you killed, and also taken possession?" (1 Kgs 21:19). Both were discovered and rebuked by a prophet. Both repented with fasting and acts of humility (see 1 Kgs 21:27). Both lost male offspring as a punishment for their sins (see 1 Kgs 21:21). Both became signs of Christ in His passion, for about Ahab it was said: "I saw all Israel scattered upon the mountains, as sheep that have no shepherd" (1 Kgs 22:17). Those are six distinct likenesses. Yet about David it was said that he "kept my commandments, and followed me with all his heart, doing only that which was right in my eyes" (1 Kgs 14:8); while about Ahab it was said: "There was none who sold himself to do what was evil in the sight of the Lord like Ahab. . . . He did very abominably" (1 Kgs 21:25).

If we were to compare the object of their sin, it is clear that David committed a greater crime than Ahab. For instead of taking a vineyard, he took the wife of Uriah. Moreover, David had been favored by greater graces from the Lord than Ahab, making David's sin even more inexcusable. Yet, it was David who obtained complete pardon. By this we learn that the mercy of the Lord is not restricted to the good, but even extends to those who are most wicked. Moreover, we learn that the good are not secure in their own righteousness, regardless of how greatly God has favored them.

Typology and Theology

It is important to distinguish between arguments made by way of typology and strict, theological demonstrations. In fact, only the literal sense of Scripture can be used to form strict demonstrations in theology: "No confusion follows from the many senses of sacred Scripture, since all of the senses are founded upon one sense, namely the literal sense, from which sense alone arguments may be drawn. However, such arguments may not be drawn from those things which are said according to allegory, as Augustine says in his epistle against Vincent the Donatist."[16]

But a type is taken from a spiritual sense of Scripture so that typology argues not from the literal sense of Scripture but from one of the spiritual senses of Scripture. This becomes clear once we understand what is meant by the spiritual sense of Scripture.

---

[16] St. Thomas Aquinas, *Summa Theologiae*, Ia, q.1, a.10, ad.1.

The spiritual sense of Scripture is contrasted with the literal sense of Scripture. The literal sense of Scripture is the meaning directly signified and intended by the *words* of the sacred author. In contrast, the spiritual sense is the meaning signified by the *things* which the words of the literal sense signify. For example, the word "manna" signifies a kind of bread which God provided for the people of Israel. This is the literal sense of the *word* "manna." But the bread itself, the *thing* signified by the word "manna," in turn signifies the Eucharist. So the spiritual sense of the physical manna is the Eucharist. So the spiritual sense presupposes and depends upon the literal sense.

Only Scripture can have a spiritual sense, because only Scripture is inspired by God. Both God and men can make words signify things, but only God can make things signify other things. For example, only God, the Lord of history, can arrange the history of the people of Israel to resemble clearly the journey of a soul from sin to heaven.[17]

Recall that a type is a person or thing which bears such a likeness to something else that it calls that later reality to mind and becomes a kind of sign of that later reality which is the fulfillment of the type. And so using some attribute of the type as a premise for arguing to some conclusion about the fulfillment of the type involves arguing from some person or thing to a truth about another person or thing. Thus, typology argues from the spiritual senses of Scripture. But since things can be like other things in some respects and unlike them in others, arguments from typology can never be completely certain. Nevertheless, such arguments can

---

[17] See *Summa Theologiae*, Ia, q.1, a.10, c.

provide probable evidence for some conclusion and point out the way for discovering a proper demonstration from the literal sense of Scripture as we have discussed already.

Thus, typology is not an invalid means of arguing, even if it is not the strongest kind of argument. In both the moral life and theology, one should not make the perfect the enemy of the good! Probable arguments have their place in theology as well, as Pope Leo XIII attests in his encyclical on devotion to Saint Joseph.[18] With these principles in mind, let us now turn to the person of Saint Joseph and see how we might enter more deeply into the mysteries of the things revealed by God about him through typology.

---

[18] See Leo XIII, *Quamquam Pluries*, no. 4.

Chapter 3

Old Testament Types of Saint Joseph

Type of Joseph or Type of Christ?

When identifying the Old Testament types of Saint Joseph, it is important to note that most of them are also types of Christ. This does not lessen their connection to Saint Joseph. We have noted that the same person or thing can be a type of multiple persons simultaneously, as Elijah is a type of Christ and John the Baptist. But the reality that those who are types of Saint Joseph are also types of Christ tells us something more: Saint Joseph was very much like Jesus. In fact, the Church teaches that among all men, he was the man closest to Christ.[19] It is to be expected, therefore, that any type of Saint Joseph will also be a type of Christ.

Joseph the Patriarch as a Type of Saint Joseph

Among the Old Testament types of Saint Joseph, the clearest and most informative is Joseph the patriarch, the son of Jacob the patriarch. Here are some parallels which show the many distinct likenesses between them:

---

19 See Leo XIII, *Quamquam Pluries*, no. 3.

1. They share the same name.
2. Their father has the same name: "Jacob the father of Joseph, the husband of Mary" (Mt 1:16). In fact, they are the only Josephs in the Bible whose fathers are named Jacob, which is unique.
3. God speaks to both through dreams (see Gn 37:5; Mt 1:20).
4. Both are forced to journey to Egypt (see Gn 37:28; Mt 2:14).
5. Both refuse to have relations with their master's spouse. For Joseph, the patriarch was given the opportunity to lie with the wife of his master, Potiphar, while Saint Joseph had the opportunity to have relations with Mary who had become the spouse of the Holy Spirit (see Gn 39:7–9; Mt 1:25).
6. Both are made ruler of the king's house and possessions. Joseph the patriarch was made ruler over all in Egypt (see Gn 41:40–41), while Saint Joseph was made head of the Holy Family, in charge of God's greatest goods, Jesus and Mary (see Lk 2:51).

Six distinct likenesses exist between Saint Joseph and Joseph the patriarch. With so many distinct likenesses, it is clear that Joseph the patriarch is a type of Saint Joseph and that this was intended by the Holy Spirit. Pope Leo XIII used this reasoning in his encyclical on devotion to Saint Joseph:

> You well understand, Venerable Brethren, that these considerations are confirmed by the opinion held by a large number of the Fathers, to which the sacred liturgy

> gives its sanction, that the Joseph of ancient times, son of the patriarch Jacob, was the type of Saint Joseph, and the former by his glory prefigured the greatness of the future guardian of the Holy Family. And in truth, beyond the fact that the same name—a point the significance of which has never been denied—was given to each, you well know the points of likeness that exist between them.[20]

Because the likenesses between Saint Joseph and Joseph the patriarch are so pronounced and obvious, it is clear that Joseph the patriarch is the principal type of Saint Joseph found in Scripture. Therefore, the majority of this book's argument shall employ the typology of Joseph the patriarch. Nevertheless, there are also other Old Testament figures who can be understood as types of Saint Joseph. These types will be used occasionally to draw conclusions about Saint Joseph in what follows.

Abraham as a Type of Saint Joseph

The patriarch Abraham is also a good example of a type of Saint Joseph. Consider the following likenesses between them:

1. Both were forced to take their wives to Egypt (see Gn 12:10; Mt 2:14).
2. Both treat their wife like a sister (see Gn 12:13; Mt 1:25).
3. Both permit their wife to be taken by a king as his wife (see Gn 12:15; Mt 2:18–25).

---

20 Leo XIII, *Quamquam Pluries*, no. 4.

4. Both believed that their wife would conceive and give birth miraculously (see Rom 4:18; Mt 2:24).
5. Both are fathers in a spiritual sense (see Rom 4:16).

At least five distinct likenesses between Abraham and Saint Joseph are present. Therefore, Abraham is a type of Saint Joseph.

Isaac as a type of Saint Joseph

After Abraham, we find that his son Isaac (also known as Israel) is a type of Saint Joseph. Consider these likenesses between them:

1. God spoke to both in dreams (see Gn 26:24; Mt 1:20).
2. Both treated their wives as sisters (see Gn 26:7; Mt 1:25).
3. Both were forced to sojourn with their wives in a foreign land (see Gn 26:1; Mt 2:14).
4. Both required God's help for their wife to conceive and bear a son (see Gn 25:21; Mt 1:20).

Isaac has at least four distinct likenesses to Saint Joseph, which is a clear indication that he is also a type of Saint Joseph.

Jacob as a type of Saint Joseph

We can see that Jacob the patriarch, grandson of Abraham, is also a good example of a type of Saint Joseph. Consider the following likenesses between them:

1. God spoke to both in dreams (see Gn 28:12; Mt 1:20).
2. Both took their families to Egypt (see Gn 46:6; Mt 2:14).
3. Both had a son who would be proclaimed the savior of the world (see Gn 41:45; Jn 4:42).
4. Both required God's help for their wife to conceive and bear a son (see Gn 30:2, 22; Mt 1:20).

Once again, there are four distinct likenesses between Jacob and Saint Joseph. It is significant that all three of the major patriarchs serve as a clear type of Saint Joseph, as seen in the next chapter. It indicates, among other things, that Saint Joseph should be considered in the line of patriarchs.

The Prophet Elijah as a Type of Joseph

One of the more intriguing types of Saint Joseph is the prophet Elijah. Consider the following likenesses:

1. Both were forced to flee towards Egypt by a ruler of Israel (see Mt 2:13; 1 Kgs 19:1–8).
2. Both lived chastely in the same home with a woman whose son would later be raised from the dead (see 1 Kgs 17).
3. An angel told both not to fear (see Mt 1:20; 2 Kgs 1:15).
4. Both were spiritual fathers, though neither was a biological father (see Lk 2:33; 2 Kgs 2:12).

Four distinct likenesses exist between Elijah and Saint Joseph with the second being particularly unique. So Elijah, too, can be called a type of Saint Joseph.

Other Possible Types of Saint Joseph

Besides those mentioned earlier, there may be other types of Saint Joseph, including Adam and King David. Adam, for example, is the husband of Eve, while Joseph is the husband of the new Eve, Mary. Moreover, Adam was the husband and father of the first natural family from which our human nature arose. And Saint Joseph is the husband and father in the Holy Family, which is first in the order of grace, and from which all of grace originates.

King David may also be a type of Saint Joseph. For example, just as David was afraid to take the Ark of the Covenant into his home (see 1 Chr 13:12), so Joseph was afraid to take the true Ark of the Covenant, Mary, into his home. And David's son Solomon was a figure of Christ, but Joseph's son Jesus was the Christ. While these cases are not as clear as the other patriarchs, nevertheless, they provide an opportunity for further reflection on other possible likenesses between Adam, King David, and Saint Joseph.

There are also a handful of other Josephs throughout Scripture who, based upon the scarcity of the name Joseph, are candidates as a type, or at least a figure, of Saint Joseph. For example, there is Joseph, son of Zechariah, mentioned as one of the leaders of the army in First and Second Maccabees. There is also Joseph the grandfather of Judith (see Jdt 8). Another Joseph in the Old Testament is Joseph, the priestly head of the family of Shebaniah (see Neh 12). In the New Testament, Barnabas is also named Joseph (see Acts 4); the alternate candidate to Matthias for filling the office of Apostle left vacant by Judas Iscariot was named Joseph (see Acts 1); and, finally, there are the two Josephs listed in Saint Luke's genealogy of Jesus: Joseph, the son of Mattathias, and Joseph the son of Jonam (see Lk 3). But because of the paucity of information we have about most of these Josephs (with the exception of Barnabas), it is unlikely that they are significant types or figures of Saint Joseph.

Chapter 4

The Significance of the Name Joseph[21]

The book of Genesis indicates, as it does with so many names, the meaning of the name Joseph. In contrast to the way in which most modern English speakers impose a name, the meaning of a name was extremely important for the ancient Hebrews and was often the determining factor of which name would be given to a child. The name of Joseph is no exception: "Then God remembered Rachel, and God hearkened to her and opened her womb. She conceived and bore a son, and said, 'God has taken away my reproach'; and she called his name Joseph, saying, 'May the Lord add to me another son!'" (Gn 30:22–24).

While the two sayings of Rachel seem to have little connection in English, they are clearly related in Hebrew. The two verbs "take away" and "may he add" are respectively *aseph* and *yoseph*, which are not only near homonyms but also etymologically related. *Yoseph* also includes meanings such as "to increase," "to grow" or "to repeat." *Aseph* can

[21] I want to acknowledge and thank Dr. Christopher DeCaen for many of the insights in this chapter. See especially his article "Joseph, the Gentiles and the Messiah," *The Aquinas Review* 22 (2017–18), 83–130.

also mean "to take up," "to gather up," or "to collect." And while *yoseph* is the exact homonym to Joseph, *aseph* is clearly intended by Rachel as well, hence the mention of both in the context of naming Joseph.

The immediate context of this passage fairly clearly manifests Rachel's intent regarding the name of Joseph the patriarch. Rachel and Leah were in a kind of competition to provide sons to Jacob. Leah was well in the lead before Rachel, who had been infertile for nearly ten years, finally had her own son. Rachel's anguish was so great at seeing her sister produce son after son that she cries out to Jacob at one point: "Give me children, or I shall die!" (Gn 30:1). Such words seem strangely prophetic since she in fact dies after having her second son (see Gn 35:18).

So in its immediate context, the desire for another son was in some way envy towards her sister, who seemed to have a greater claim on Jacob's love because she provided him with many sons. And the reproach which was taken away was the reproach of not having provided her husband with any sons. From a broader perspective, the desire to provide many sons to Jacob was in order to fulfill the promise made to Abraham, Isaac, and Jacob that their descendants would be numerous as the stars of heaven and that all the nations would find blessing in their offspring. As it turns out, Joseph seems to outdo his brothers in this regard, since from him issued Ephraim and Manasseh, who became two of the principal tribes of Israel. Indeed, the ten tribes of the north are sometimes just called Ephraim or Joseph, just as the southern two tribes are often referred to as Judah:

> Son of man, take a stick and write on it, 'For Judah, and the children of Israel associated with him'; then take another stick and write upon it, 'For Joseph (the stick of Ephraim) and all the house of Israel associated with him'; and join them together into one stick, that they may become one in your hand. . . . Say to them, Thus says the Lord God: Behold, I am about to take the stick of Joseph (which is in the hand of Ephraim) and the tribes of Israel associated with him; and I will join with it the stick of Judah, and make them one stick, that they may be one in my hand. (Ez 37:16–17, 19)

Throughout the other prophets and histories as well, the northern kingdom is referred to simply as Ephraim, as if to indicate that they were more numerous and important than all the other nine tribes of the north.[22] This is expressly stated in Jacob's blessing of Ephraim: "[Manasseh's] younger brother shall be greater than he, and his descendants shall become a multitude of nations" (Gn 48:19). The promise concerning a multitude of nations refers back, of course, to the promise made by God to Abraham, Isaac, and Jacob. So Joseph seems to have *added* to the number of the chosen people even more than his brethren.[23] Not only that but Joseph also *adds* the Egyptian people to the chosen race, which seems to be the beginning of the fulfillment of the second part of God's promise "in your seed all the nations of the earth shall find

---

[22] See, for example, Is 7; Jer 31; Hos 5 and 9; and 2 Chr 25.

[23] Thus, in the census recorded in the book of Numbers, chapter 26, the descendants of Joseph outnumber the descendants of the other sons of Jacob by a wide margin (Joseph's descendants numbered 85,200 while the next closest was Judah with 76,500).

blessing" (Gn 22:18). In fact, we find that towards the end of Genesis, Jacob adopts his half-Egyptian sons Ephraim and Manasseh as his own: "[Jacob said] and now your two sons, who were born to you in the land of Egypt before I came to you in Egypt, are mine; Ephraim and Manasseh shall be mine, as Reuben and Simeon are. And the offspring born to you after them shall be yours; they shall be called by the name of their brothers in their inheritance" (Gn 48:5–6).

So these sons of Joseph of Egyptian heritage are added to the tribes of Israel and counted among them as equal sharers in the blessing, as if they had been sons born to Jacob himself.

From these considerations, we can see that the name Joseph has a prophetic meaning, extending beyond Rachel's desire to add to her sons for the sake of pleasing Jacob. Joseph's name refers mysteriously to the promise made by God to Abraham, Isaac, and Jacob not only to multiply their offspring but to bless all the nations of the earth through their seed.

This brings us to Saint Joseph. Saint Joseph's name appears for the first time in the New Testament at the conclusion of the genealogy of Saint Matthew's Gospel (see Mt 1:16). It is worth noting that the title of the Gospel according to Matthew is actually the "Book of the Genesis (γενέσεως) of Jesus Christ." Of course, this would naturally call to mind the book of Genesis of the Septuagint text commonly used by the Jews of Saint Matthew's time. And just as the book of Genesis ends with the person of Joseph, the genealogy, or genesis, given by Matthew ends with Saint Joseph.

Notice that all three of the great patriarchs—Abraham, Isaac, and Jacob—are types of Saint Joseph, as we saw in the last chapter. Now to each of these three patriarchs, God reiterated His promise to multiply their offspring and bless all the nations of the earth through their seed (see Gn 22:18; Gn 26:3–4; Gn 28:13–14). Notice too that each of them had a wife who needed divine intervention in order to conceive and bear a son. This was to underscore the fact that God's intervention was continuously necessary for the fulfillment of the promise. Yet none of these three patriarchs saw the perfect fulfillment of the promise. While they received carnal offspring by God's help, it was only Saint Joseph who would call that Offspring in whom the nations of the earth would find blessing his own son. While the wives of Abraham, Isaac, and Jacob required divine intervention to beget offspring by their husbands, the wife of Joseph would require divine intervention of a higher order in order to conceive and bear a child without the cooperation of any man.

All of this was to foreshadow the fact that Joseph, the ultimate patriarch, would be the inheritor of the great promise made to each of them separately: "in your offspring will the nations be blessed." But just as the promise was fulfilled in a manner much greater than some earthly blessing, so too the generation of that Offspring would be accomplished in a manner beyond the physical or carnal. Thus, it is not carnal generation but birth in the Spirit which produces offspring of Abraham and the fulfillment of the promise made by God to Abraham, Isaac, and Jacob. This is something Jesus Himself taught (see Mt 3:9; Jn 8:39). And Saint Paul made this insight a central aspect of his teaching on justification: "Not all who are descended from Israel belong to Israel, and not all are children of Abraham because they are his descendants;

but 'Through Isaac shall your descendants be named.' This means that it is not the children of the flesh who are the children of God, but the children of the promise are reckoned as descendants" (Rom 9:6–8).

And again:

> Thus Abraham "believed God, and it was credited to him as righteousness." So you see that it is men of faith who are the sons of Abraham. And the scripture, foreseeing that God would justify the Gentiles by faith, preached the gospel beforehand to Abraham, saying, "In you shall all the nations be blessed." So then, those who are men of faith are blessed with Abraham who had faith. . . . Christ redeemed us from the curse of the law, having become a curse for us—for it is written, "Cursed be every one who hangs on a tree"—that in Christ Jesus the blessing of Abraham might come upon the Gentiles, that we might receive the promise of the Spirit through faith. (Gal 3:6–9, 13–14)[24]

By studying divine revelation, we can uncover the deeper meaning of the name Joseph. The name Joseph refers to the taking away (*aseph*) of the reproach of the sin of our race and the adding (*yoseph*) of the Son of God to our race, as well as the adding of the nations to God's people in the Church. Although implicit, Saint Joseph's desire for the coming of the Messiah was so great that it is expressed by his name.

---

[24] Cf. Rom 4.

Chapter 5

The Holiness of Saint Joseph

Perhaps the first point we should address is the question of Saint Joseph's proximity to Jesus; in other words, his degree of holiness. The eminent sanctity of Saint Joseph has been admitted by Christians down throughout the ages. But the degree of Saint Joseph's sanctity relative to the other saints had been an open question for centuries. For example, the words of Jesus concerning Saint John the Baptist seemed to be an assertion that Saint John the Baptist held the highest place in heaven after Our Lady: "I tell you, among those born of women none is greater than John" (Lk 7:28). It is only in recent times that the magisterium of the Catholic Church has settled the question of the relative priority of Saint Joseph to the other saints, after the Blessed Virgin Mary: "There can be no doubt but that Joseph approached as no other person ever could that eminent dignity whereby the Mother of God towers above all creatures."[25]

What is the evidence given for Saint Joseph's preeminence among the saints? The principal arguments for this conclusion center upon Saint Joseph's unique relationship to Mary and Jesus, as well as upon his exalted mission from

[25] Pope Saint John Paul II, *Redemptoris Custos* no. 20.

God concerning them. We can also add arguments from the types of Saint Joseph discussed above.

Pope Leo XIII argues both from Saint Joseph's relationship to Mary as her spouse, and to Jesus as His guardian: "The special motives for which St. Joseph has been proclaimed Patron of the Church, and from which the Church looks for singular benefit from his patronage and protection, are that Joseph was the spouse of Mary and that he was reputed the father of Jesus Christ. From these sources have sprung his dignity, his holiness, his glory."[26]

After mentioning the two sources of Saint Joseph's dignity, Pope Leo argues for Saint Joseph's eminent dignity from his spousal relationship to Mary:

> In truth, the dignity of the Mother of God is so lofty that naught created can rank above it. But as Joseph has been united to the Blessed Virgin by the ties of marriage, it may not be doubted that he approached nearer than any to the eminent dignity by which the Mother of God surpasses so nobly all created natures. For marriage is the most intimate of all unions which from its essence imparts a community of gifts between those that by it are joined together. Thus in giving Joseph the Blessed Virgin as spouse, God appointed him to be not only her life's companion, the witness of her maidenhood, the protector of her honor, but also, by virtue of the conjugal tie, a participator in her sublime dignity.[27]

---

[26] Pope Leo XIII, *Quamquam Pluries*, no. 3.

[27] Pope Leo XIII, *Quamquam Pluries*, no. 3.

Based upon the nature and purpose of marriage, it is evident that marriage demands a sharing of lives and goods. For marriage is, by definition, a kind of communion of persons. In fact, the child itself is shared as a common good of the spouses. And it is evident from Scripture that Saint Joseph did not fall short of the demands of marriage. The Scriptures portray him as being docile and obedient to God's will even as expressed in dreams. He cared for Mary and Jesus to the point of total sacrifice, believing, with the love that believes all things, in the chastity of his pregnant wife and fleeing to Egypt where he had no work or close relations. Nor should we underestimate the power of the Virgin Mary's constant prayers made for the man to whom she owed the greatest gratitude. Finally, since Mary was subject to Joseph as her husband, and since her every action was a source of grace, present and future, for the whole Church, it was necessary that Saint Joseph be granted a sanctity of sufficient loftiness that his direction of the Virgin contribute always and everywhere to the benefit of the Church and the salvation of souls.

Next, Pope Leo argues to Saint Joseph's eminent dignity based upon his relationship to Jesus: "And Joseph shines among all mankind by the most august dignity, since by divine will, he was the guardian of the Son of God and reputed as His father among men. Hence it came about that the Word of God was humbly subject to Joseph, that He obeyed him, and that He rendered to him all those offices that children are bound to render to their parents."[28]

---

[28] Pope Leo XIII, *Quamquam Pluries*, no. 3.

By a mysterious decree of the divine will, Saint Joseph was appointed the guardian of the Son of God, though Jesus needed no one to protect Him from dangers or provide for Him. He could have exercised His divine power to protect and provide for His human nature better than any creature could have done. Yet, in His wisdom, the Son of God refused to perform any miracle to protect or provide for Himself. For when His apostles sought to defend Him by the sword from His impending passion, Jesus rebuked them saying, "Put your sword back into its place; for all who take the sword will perish by the sword. Do you think that I cannot appeal to my Father, and he will at once send me more than twelve legions of angels?"(Mt 26:52–53). So too, when Herod threatened Him, He performed no miracle, but rather trusted in Saint Joseph to guard Him. And when He was hungry or thirsty, He waited upon the loving providence of a human father in order to obtain what was necessary for His life. So it was that in the actual order of things, Jesus depended upon Joseph.

Pope Leo adds that Joseph was "reputed as His father among men."[29] As Jesus's father, it fell to Joseph to be the

---

[29] At this point, it is appropriate to defend the language I shall use going forward in this text concerning Saint Joseph's fatherhood of Jesus. Often, it is customary to refer to Saint Joseph as the "foster father" of Jesus. The motives for this language are obvious: Jesus does not have a natural human father. He was conceived of a virgin, and so God the Father is His only natural Father. True as this is, it is a mistake to use this as a reason to relegate Saint Joseph to the status of "foster father," which in the English language has connotations much like stepfather. Terms like "foster father" and "stepfather" connote a sense of apparent or false fatherhood: someone who is just a placeholder for a real dad but who doesn't think of or care about the child as if it were his own. When a man adopts a child,

first to call Jesus by His name (see Mt 1:21, 25). This is itself astounding, since in the Old Testament, to confer a name on someone indicates authority over and knowledge of the one to whom the name is given, as Adam conferred a name upon each of the animals, and even upon his own wife, Eve. Moreover, God's name was so holy and sacred that it was hidden from all but the greatest saints, and when at last it was revealed, it was not to be spoken except once a year by the high priest. And it was God who gave a name to these great ones, such as Abraham and Israel. But here a man calls the Son of God by His name and gives to other men the name by which the Son of God is to be called.

The truth that Joseph was reputed as the father of Jesus before men also means that Joseph received the effective grace to love Jesus as his own son, and that Jesus, besides having a filial affection and piety, honored and was subject to Joseph. It is a difficult thing to love God well without the further complication of loving God as if He were your own child. Yet to Saint Joseph was given the miraculous grace not only

---

his children don't call him foster father, or even adoptive father. They call him dad. If we turn to the Scriptures, we find that Saint Joseph is not called the "foster father" of Jesus. Instead, we find Mary simply referring to Joseph as his "father" (Lk 2:48). And Saint Luke himself, inspired by the Holy Spirit, simply calls him "his father" (Lk 2:33). While biological fatherhood is better known to us, nevertheless, to be a spiritual father is to be a father simply speaking, not in some diminished respect. If this were not the case, then even God's fatherhood would be qualified and diminished. Yet Saint Paul says the opposite (see Eph 3:14–15). Following the usage of Sacred Scripture, therefore, I will simply refer to Saint Joseph as the father of Jesus. There is no danger in the context of this work for anyone to think that by this appellation, I am asserting that Jesus was begotten biologically by a natural, human father.

to love God with his whole mind, heart, soul, and strength but to be an image of the heavenly Father in His love for His Only-Begotten Son, a grace granted to no other creature save Saint Joseph. In his human soul and imagination, the image of father which Jesus acquired from His experience was the image of Saint Joseph. And when He thought of God His Father, that thought was always bound up with the human understanding of father He associated with Saint Joseph.

Finally, the Scriptures assert, Jesus was obedient to Joseph (see Lk 2:51). It is certain that Jesus obeyed the will of Joseph perfectly. Consider that every action of Christ had infinite value and contributed to the salvation of the world. With His every action, Jesus was accomplishing the salvation of souls. Yet those actions were often determined by the will of Saint Joseph. Therefore, Saint Joseph must have received grace in such abundance that never did he compromise in the least the salvation of souls. What divine light and love must have dwelt in that holy soul as he guided the Savior of the world and the King of the universe to bring about the greatest common good of all the elect.

Last of all, Pope Leo deduces that Saint Joseph, in virtue of his relationship to Mary and Jesus, had the responsibility to care for the Holy Family: "From this two-fold dignity flowed the obligation which nature lays upon the head of families, so that Joseph became the guardian, the administrator, and the legal defender of the divine house whose chief he was. And during the whole course of his life he fulfilled those charges and those duties."[30]

---

[30] Pope Leo XIII, *Quamquam Pluries*, no. 3.

Joseph was the head of the Holy Family, which was the whole of the Church in seminal form and power. In other words, Joseph tended to the common good of his family upon which depended the good of the entire human family. From these considerations, it is clear that Saint Joseph, after Mary, holds the highest dignity in heaven, and surpasses all the other saints in holiness. And it can be asserted with certitude now who it is that sits at the right and the left hand of the Savior at the heavenly banquet. We can also guess why Jesus said it was not His to give, but His Father in heaven (see Mt 20:23); for these were His parents, and in filial humility, He desired not that He should confer the honor but that His Father in heaven do so.

The Question of Saint John the Baptist

We should return to Jesus's words concerning Saint John the Baptist. For the clearer texts in Scripture should govern our interpretation of those which are less clear. And it seems that Jesus has asserted plainly and unequivocally that Saint John the Baptist was the holiest among the saints: "I tell you, among those born of women none is greater than John" (Lk 7:28); and again: "Truly, I say to you, among those born of women there has risen no one greater than John the Baptist" (Mt 11:11). If Jesus states clearly that John is the greatest among the saints, then the arguments we have given above concerning Saint Joseph should be rejected in favor of the clear words of Christ.

However, what initially seems to be a clear statement by Jesus concerning Saint John the Baptist's relative holiness and dignity above the other saints turns out to be a statement which Jesus Himself qualifies by adding, "Yet he who is least in the kingdom of heaven is greater than he" (Mt 11:11). If the least in the kingdom of heaven is greater than John, and undoubtedly there are saints in the kingdom of heaven, then there must be saints who are greater than John.

How, then, are we to understand Jesus's original statement about John? One way to interpret Jesus's words about His cousin is to understand them as applying to John according to his natural gifts (for example, as regards intelligence and charisma). This fits with Jesus specifying "among those born of women." For it is by our natural birth that we receive the inheritance of human nature and its attendant gifts. Another way to interpret Jesus's words about John is to refer them to John's gift of prophecy and his rank among the Old Testament prophets. This interpretation is suggested by Jesus's words which follow in Saint Matthew's Gospel: "All the prophets and the law prophesied until John" (11:13). All the prophets saw Christ as the one who was to come, but those in the kingdom of heaven see the fulfillment of prophecy in the Christ who has already come. Certainly, John too saw the Christ who had already come, not as a prophet, but as one who receives the reward promised to the prophets. However one interprets this saying of Jesus, it is clear that he is not asserting that there are no saints of greater holiness than John the Baptist.

Chapter 6

Virginal Spouse of Mary

In this chapter, I intend to consider the question of whether Saint Joseph, like Mary, was a virgin. No faithful Catholic has ever claimed that Saint Joseph ever had relations with Mary. So that is not the question I am addressing here. Rather, the question I am addressing here is whether Saint Joseph had been married and had children prior to his marriage to the Blessed Virgin Mary.

To my knowledge, there are two reasons why this has been somewhat of a controversial question in the history of the Church. The first reason is that some early commentators on the Gospels attempted to solve the problem that Jesus is said to have brothers and sisters by claiming that these are actually children of Saint Joseph from a previous marriage.[31] The second reason is that Saint Joseph is sometimes portrayed

[31] These passages include Mk 3:31, Mk 6:3, and Mt 13:55–56. Some apocryphal sources and Eastern Fathers of the Church assert that Saint Joseph had other children prior to his union with Mary. For example, the Protoevangelium of James, the Gospel of Pseudo-Matthew, the Coptic history of Joseph the Carpenter, and the Gospel of Thomas are all apocrypha (non-canonical writings) which claim that Joseph had a previous marriage and was an older man. Among the Fathers of the Church who adopted this position were Epiphanius, Gregory of Nyssa, Ephrem, and Hilary. These opinions have never been adopted as Church teaching.

as an older man when he married Our Lady. Now, it would have been almost unthinkable for an older man not to have been married in the time of Saint Joseph, especially since it was seen as a moral obligation to increase the number of God's people and hasten the coming of the Messiah. So from the supposition that Saint Joseph was an old man, some have concluded that he had been previously married.

First, I will address both of these reasons to show that they are not conclusive. Second, I will manifest from the New Testament sources, as well as from the principal types of Saint Joseph, that he was indeed a virgin throughout his entire lifetime.

The first argument given for the position that Saint Joseph had other children from a prior marriage is based upon the supposition that the brothers and sisters of Jesus mentioned in the Gospels of Mark and Matthew are brothers and sisters (*adelphos*) in the strictest sense of the word—that is, people having the same immediate parent. But in fact, the term *adelphos* as used in the Greek language in the time of the New Testament had several meanings which extend beyond the strictest meaning. For example, the term is used elsewhere in the New Testament to refer to cousins, and even to members of the same religion. How then can we know which sense Matthew and Mark used? The answer is simple. If we compare several passages in Matthew's and John's Gospels, we discover that the same people who are called Jesus's brothers in one text are expressly identified as the children of His mother's sister in another text (see Jn 19, Mt 13). Thus, the term *adelphos* when referring to Jesus's brothers and sisters must mean cousins. This also means that they were not Joseph's children. Hence the assertion that Joseph had children from a previous marriage falls apart when carefully reading the whole of Scripture.

In fact, Saint Jerome addressed the false claim that Saint Joseph had other children:

> Certain people who follow the ravings of the apocrypha fancy that the brethren of the Lord are sons of Joseph from another wife, and invent a certain woman, Melcha or Escha. As it is contained in the book which we wrote against Helvidius, we understand as brethren of the Lord not the sons of Joseph but the cousins of the Savior, children of Mary [of Clopas] the Lord's maternal aunt, who is said to be the mother of James the Less, and Joseph and Jude. They, as we read, were called brethren of the Lord in another passage of the Gospel. Indeed, all Scripture indicates that cousins are called brethren.[32]

And in another place, Saint Jerome wrote: "You say that Mary did not remain a virgin; even more do I claim that Joseph was also virginal through Mary, in order that from a virginal marriage a virginal son might be born. For if the charge of fornication does not fall upon this holy man, and if it is not written that he had another wife, and if he was more protector than a husband of Mary, whom he was thought to have as a wife, it remains to assert that he who merited to be called the father of the Lord remained virginal with her."[33]

---

[32] *Commentary on Matthew*, ch. 12.

[33] *Against Helvidius*, 10.

The second reason for the position that Saint Joseph was previously married is the supposition that Joseph was already an elderly man at the time of his marriage to Mary. The origins of this tradition are found in apocryphal literature but not in Sacred Scripture. Many of the original traditions surrounding Saint Joseph were likely concerned about guarding the virginal nature of his marriage to Mary. One way to represent this to popular imagination would have involved portraying Saint Joseph as much older than Mary, more of a father figure than a husband. This would reduce the chance of ordinary Christians casting suspicion upon his chastity. Conveniently, Saint Joseph seems to have died before Jesus reached the age of thirty, lending further credence to the "old Saint Joseph" narrative. But what does Sacred Scripture say upon the matter?

The first clear indication that Saint Joseph was a young man involved the Holy Family's flight into Egypt. To escape King Herod's impending slaughter, Saint Joseph set off in the night, at times carrying the infant God in his arms. Old men do not walk to Egypt, especially a trek of hundreds of miles in the desert on such short notice (and hence with limited supplies). It is true that some older men made long journeys in the ancient world. But in those cases, they had time to make provisions and traveled by caravan, usually riding an animal or being carried by servants. So the circumstances of Saint Joseph's journey to Egypt indicate that he was a young man.

There is also another indication in the Scriptures which suggests that Saint Joseph was a young man. There are many words in the Greek language of the New Testament which can be used to signify a male human being. In Luke 1:27, the word used to describe Joseph was ανδρι. According to lexographical studies, this term signifies a man in his prime.[34] If Saint Joseph had been a middle-aged or elderly man, it is likely that Saint Luke would have used the Greek term πρεσβύτης as he did when referring to Zachary (Lk 1:18).

Saint Thomas Aquinas also thought that Sacred Scripture teaches that Saint Joseph was a young man. He states this in his commentary on the prophet Isaiah. Commenting upon the passage in Isaiah 62, which reads "the young man shall dwell with the virgin," Saint Thomas writes, "In the mystical sense the young man dwelling chastely with the virgin refers to Mary living with Joseph."[35]

Finally, Saint Thomas offers another reason Saint Joseph was a young man: his role in guarding the secret of the Incarnation. One of the reasons why Mary was espoused to Saint Joseph at the time of the conception of Jesus was to hide this virginal conception from the devil: "It was fitting that Christ was to be born of a married virgin . . . for the sake of the defense of the child, lest the devil attempt to harm him more vehemently. And, therefore, Ignatius says that 'she was married so that his birth might be hidden from the devil.'"[36] But an old man would not have hidden the miraculous nature of Christ's conception from the devil very well since it would not be likely that such an old man could beget a son.

---

[34] Philo of Alexandria is one example of an ancient authority who expressly taught this position.

[35] *Commentary on Isaiah* 62.

[36] *Summa Theologiae*, IIIa, q.29, a.1, c. (Also, see St. Jerome's commentary on Matthew, book I.)

It is clear from all of these reasons, rooted in Sacred Scripture and Tradition, that Saint Joseph was certainly a young man. And if he was a young man, there is no reason to suppose that he had been previously married. Let us now turn to the evidence from typology that Saint Joseph was a virgin throughout his life.

Typological Evidence that Saint Joseph Was a Virgin

Among the clearest types of Saint Joseph, we find none who remained a virgin. Abraham, Isaac, Jacob, and Joseph all married and begot children of their own. And this is to be expected since the virginity of Saint Joseph was in immediate preparation for the coming of the new dispensation in Christ. Indeed, it seems to have been the belief among most Israelites that by having as many children as possible, they would hasten the coming of the Messiah. Little did they suspect that the parents of the Messiah would both be virgins!

Given that none of Saint Joseph's clear types were themselves virgins, what evidence can we find in them for Saint Joseph's virginity? In each person who is a type of Saint Joseph, we find some attribute that suggests celibacy or sexual abstinence. Let us examine Saint Joseph's clear types individually.

Among the distinct likenesses we find between Abraham and Saint Joseph, there are three which can be interpreted typologically to imply some kind of celibacy. First, both Abraham and Joseph treat their wife like a sister. In Genesis 12:13, we read that Abraham said to Sarah, his wife, "Say you are my sister, that it may go well with me because of you, and that my life may be spared on your account." But treating a wife like a sister implies living together without sexual intercourse. Second, both Abraham and Joseph permit their wife to be taken by a king as his wife. Thus, we read in Genesis 12:15: "And when the princes of Pharaoh saw [Sarah], they praised her to Pharaoh. And the woman was taken into Pharaoh's house." But allowing a wife to be taken as the spouse of another once again implies celibacy on the part of the original husband. Finally, both Abraham and Joseph believed that their wives would conceive and give birth miraculously. For example, it is written in Romans 4:19 that "[Abraham] did not weaken in faith when he considered his own body, which was as good as dead because he was about a hundred years old, or when he considered the barrenness of Sarah's womb." Because a miracle is necessary to conceive a child (for those who follow Church teaching) implies that God is the true and primary agent in the conception of that child. This in turn opens the possibility of God causing the conception without the cooperation of any human father, as happened in the case of the Blessed Virgin Mary. In some way, Saint Joseph's virginity is foreshadowed or typified in each of these likenesses between Abraham and Saint Joseph.

Let us turn now to Isaac and see what elements of his life imply that Saint Joseph was a virgin. Recall that Isaac imitated his father Abraham when he sojourned in the land of the Philistines. Out of fear, he told them that Rebecca was his sister: "When the men of the place asked questions about his wife, he said, 'She is my sister'; for he feared to say, 'My wife,' thinking, 'lest the men of the place should kill me for the sake of Rebekah'; because she was fair to look upon" (Gn 26:7). Once again, to dwell with one's wife as if with a sister implies that they are not engaging in sexual intercourse. So it is clear how this event in the life of Isaac is a type of the virginity of Saint Joseph. Moreover, both Isaac and Joseph required God's help for their wives to conceive and bear sons. Thus, we read in Genesis 25:21: "Isaac prayed to the Lord for his wife, because she was barren; and the Lord granted his prayer, and Rebecca his wife conceived." Thus the primary agent in the conception of Rebecca's children is God, not a human father. This can be read typologically to indicate that Saint Joseph would not be the agent of conception of the Son of Mary.

Turning now to the person of Jacob, we find in his life, too, an element that can be interpreted to typify the virginity of Saint Joseph. As with Abraham and Isaac, Jacob also requires God's help for his wife to conceive and bear a son. In Genesis 30:1–2, we read, "When Rachel saw that she bore Jacob no children, she envied her sister; and she said to Jacob: 'Give me children, or I shall die!' Jacob's anger was kindled against Rachel, and he said, 'Am I in the place of God, who has withheld from you the fruit of the womb?'" Notice that Jacob states that God is the primary cause in conceiving a child. This again points to the future conception of Jesus by God's sole agency. Furthermore, in Genesis 30:22–23, we read, "Then God remembered Rachel, and God hearkened to her and opened her womb. She conceived and bore a son." That son was indeed Joseph. Notice that the text does not say that Jacob knew his wife and that she bore him a son. That is true. But the sacred author focuses again on God's agency by making Jacob a clearer type of Saint Joseph's virginity.

Finally, let us consider Joseph the patriarch to see whether his life typifies Saint Joseph's virginity. Genesis 39:7–9 holds the key. In this text, we see a likeness between the two Josephs: both refuse to have relations with their master's spouse. Joseph the patriarch refuses to have relations with the spouse of Potiphar, and Saint Joseph refused to have relations with the spouse of the Holy Spirit:

> Now Joseph was handsome and good-looking. And after a time his master's wife cast her eyes upon Joseph, and said, "Lie with me." But he refused and said to his master's wife, "Lo, having me my master has no concern about anything in the house, and he has put everything that he has in my hand; he is not greater in this house than I am; nor has he kept back anything from me except yourself, because you are his wife; how then can I do this great wickedness, and sin against God?"

Here Joseph gives a reason he cannot have intercourse with the wife of his master: namely, because his master has shown great trust in him and great generosity. Moreover, it would have been a sin of adultery before God. Therefore, we find an element in the life of Joseph which can be interpreted as a type of Saint Joseph's virginity.

When interpreting this passage as a type of Saint Joseph's virginity, an obvious objection can be raised. If this passage is a type of Saint Joseph's proposal to remain a virgin, then the wife of Potiphar represents the Virgin Mary. But it is unthinkable that Mary would ever try to seduce or tempt Saint Joseph.

To answer this objection, it is important to realize that not every type is a likeness in every respect. There is a saying in philosophy: every analogy limps. For if an analogy were the same in every respect, it would no longer be an analogy but the same thing. Something similar might be said about a biblical type: if it were alike in every respect, it would not be a type but the very same reality. So how might we interpret the role of the wife of Potiphar as a type of Mary in this case? Insofar as Saint Joseph had a human nature which is naturally inclined to reproduce with a member of the opposite sex, and insofar as Saint Joseph had this right because he was truly married to the Virgin Mary, we can say that Saint Joseph had to resist the natural inclination to have intercourse with his wife, Mary, on account of a higher good which God had revealed to him. So in that sense, there was a "temptation" for Joseph: not a deliberate or chosen temptation caused by Mary, but a natural temptation because Mary was his wife. She was intrinsically the object of a natural desire, but it was a natural desire which had to be resisted on account of a greater, supernatural good. Something similar might be said about any priest who is vowed to virginity: he must resist the natural desire to marry on account of a greater, supernatural good. Saint Joseph was so imbued with a supernatural spirit that he overcame the temptation arising from his natural inclinations without any sin.

Reflecting on the clearest types of Saint Joseph, we notice that all of them either required their spouse to conceive with God's help or had to treat their spouse as a sister or the spouse of another. The most reasonable conclusion is that these types point to the virginity of Saint Joseph.

The Prophet Elijah

While none of the aforementioned patriarchs lived expressly as a virgin, there is still one type of Saint Joseph that we have not yet mentioned. It is the prophet Elijah. Recall that Elijah lived for years with a widow and her son. This is clear evidence that Elijah did not have a family of his own. Hence, we have a type of Saint Joseph who did remain a virgin throughout his life. This is also confirmed by the spiritual fatherhood he exercised towards Elisha the prophet.

The home of Elijah, the widow, and her son (who would later be raised from the dead) also can be seen as a clear type of the chaste and virginal home of the Holy Family. So in the person of Elijah, we have the clearest typological evidence for the virginity of Saint Joseph. We are now in a better position to examine the biblical evidence for this same position from the literal sense of Scripture.

Theological Demonstration that Saint Joseph Was a Virgin

Even without the benefit of typology, there is strong evidence that Saint Joseph, like Our Lady, had made a lifelong promise to God to remain a virgin. I will provide two arguments for this position.

The first is an argument from fittingness. Just as the conception of Jesus was virginal, so too it was right that the marriage in which that conception took place be virginal.

For a virgin ought to be cared for and protected by a virgin. Thus, at the end of his life, Jesus entrusted Mary to another virgin: John the Apostle. Even the pagans recognized this fact, so they entrusted the virgins of the harem of the king to eunuchs (see Est 2:3). This argument was made by Saint Jerome, and later expanded upon by Saint Thomas in his commentary on Matthew 12:

> Since he makes mention of brothers, therefore, this text has been the occasion of heresy: that when the Virgin had given birth to Jesus, Joseph knew Mary and begot children thereafter. But this is heretical, since after the birth of Jesus, the Virgin remained inviolate. So there was also the opinion that these sons were of Joseph from another wife. But this is not so since we believe that just as the mother of Jesus was a virgin, so also Joseph, since [God] entrusted a virgin to a virgin. And just as at the end [of Jesus's life] so also at the beginning.[37]

Again, Saint Thomas makes the same argument in his commentary on Galatians:

> But others say that Joseph had another wife before the Blessed Virgin, from whom he had a son, Jacob, and the others. But when that wife died, he took the Blessed Virgin as his wife, of whom was born the Christ, but not by knowing Joseph, but through the Holy Spirit, as is said in the Gospel. Therefore, since relations are named from the father's side, and Joseph

---

[37] Super Ev. Matt., 12, lect. 4.

> was reputed to be the father of Christ, therefore, this Jacob, although he was not the son of the Virgin, nevertheless was called the brother of the Lord. But this is false, since if the Lord only willed to commend his virgin mother to the care of a virgin [John], how could he have endured that her spouse was not a virgin, and to remain in this condition?[38]

One way to think about this is to ask a simple question: If Saint Joseph was not a virgin but had been accustomed to have relations with his previous wife, how could he have lived with Mary without sin, or at least the near occasion of sin through grave temptations? But if Joseph had already proposed to live as a virgin, this showed his self-mastery and that he had sufficient spiritual maturity to remain in a marriage with the Blessed Virgin without placing himself in a near occasion of sin.

This line of thinking leads us to the next argument which seems to conclusively demonstrate that Saint Joseph was a virgin throughout his lifetime. If Mary had already promised virginity to God and still entered into marriage with Joseph, then this could only have been on the condition that she knew that Saint Joseph too had promised a life of virginity. For it would have been a sin to give to someone the right over her body for acts apt to generate children (and this is what everyone who marries does) and yet to deny that very right on account of a prior promise to God. But, of course, it is impossible that the Blessed Virgin Mary sinned by entering into a marriage with Saint Joseph. Therefore, Saint

---

[38] In Ep. Gal., c.1, lect. 5.

Joseph (or God) must have already revealed to her that he intended to remain a virgin throughout his entire lifetime. Saint Thomas makes this very argument, concluding that "neither did Mary have another son, nor did Joseph, since he too was a virgin."[39] Saint Thomas also proposes an objection, and then gives his answer:

> Someone vowing virginity exposes herself to danger if she hands herself over to the power of a husband. But this is a sin. Therefore, the Blessed Virgin ought not to have handed herself over to the power of another by marrying. And, therefore, she should not have married.
>
> The Blessed Virgin, before she had contracted marriage with Joseph was made certain by divine revelation that Joseph had placed himself in a similar state [of vowed virginity]. And, therefore, she did not place herself in danger by marrying.[40]

Mary's response to the angel Gabriel is proof that she already promised her virginity to God. Gabriel had told her that she was to conceive and bear a son. Since she was already married, such a prediction should have posed no problem for a woman who intended to have intercourse with her husband. But the Virgin Mary instead raises the objection that she "does not know man"—that is, that she intends not to have sexual intercourse with a man. This answer is unintelligible unless she had already promised her virginity.

---

39 In IV Sent., d.30, q.2, a.3, ad.4.

40 In IV Sent., d.30, q.2, a.1b, obj.2 and resp.2.

But if she made this pledge and still entered into a true and valid marriage with Joseph, the only possible explanation for this action was that Joseph, too, had promised virginity and Mary knew about this promise.

So if one reads the New Testament text carefully, one can see that Saint Joseph's virginity is implied, and only by assuming this truth are the actions of Mary and Joseph understandable.

Joseph's Virginity a Model for Men in Every State of Life

Because Joseph has the unique status of being both a married man and a virgin, it is reasonable to ask if Saint Joseph can be a model for other men. After all, how can a virgin be a model for a married man? And how can a married man be a model for a priest or religious who has taken a vow of celibacy? It seems that Saint Joseph's special calling makes him incapable of being a model for anyone else.

But the truth is that Joseph can be a model for every man in every state of life. The reason for this is that Saint Joseph offers the supreme example of a virtue which should be common to all men in every state of life: single, married, or consecrated. And that virtue is self-mastery over the power of reproduction. What defines a male of the human species is the active ability to generate life in another. A man is someone who, when mature, ought to have the ability to beget life in another. And once that life is begotten, he has the duty to protect and foster that life. But it is also true that all men are subject to original sin. And one consequence of original sin is the disobedience of our reproductive power to reason. Often enough, we feel the urge to use our reproductive power in times or circumstances when it is unreasonable to do so. This is universal to human experience. The married man finds a woman other than his wife attractive, and so feels a temptation to use his power of reproduction with her. The man who has taken a vow of celibacy finds women attractive and is tempted to break his promise to God. The unmarried, young man desires to use his reproductive power with his girlfriend, or some other woman to whom he is not married. The list goes on and on. Therefore, every man, regardless of his state of life, ought to acquire the virtue of self-mastery over his reproductive power. Saint Joseph can be a model for every man, as well as a powerful intercessor in this matter.

Saint Joseph is a model for every married man even though he never exercised his right to sexual intercourse. When a man marries a woman, he hands over to her the right over his body for acts apt to generate children. He gives the right over his generative power to another. But someone cannot give what he does not first possess. And a man who does not have self-mastery over his generative power is not able to hand the right over this power to his wife since he does not fully possess or control that power. A man who is a slave to his sexual desires cannot always control those desires. So sometimes he will end up using his generative power without his wife's consent, or at least not in a way that respects her legitimate rights over his generative power. When a man is a slave to his sexual desires, his wife becomes a slave to those same desires, and this is extremely harmful to the sacred bond of marriage. He sometimes uses his generative power in a way that does not achieve the good of his wife and family. Saint Joseph offers a supreme example of a man who possessed control over his generative power. Though he had the right to make use of this power with his wife, he let go of this right for the sake of a higher good and vocation. For this reason, he can be compassionate towards men who are struggling to deny their lower desires in order to do the right thing.

I know of many cases where due to no fault on the husband's part, he is deprived of the legitimate use of his reproductive power. Sometimes because his wife is seriously ill, sometimes because his wife has abandoned him, sometimes because his wife refuses his reasonable requests for marital intimacy. In these instances, some husbands might say something like, "I didn't take a vow of celibacy, so I should be free to find another wife." But the truth is that every wedding vow is potentially a vow of celibacy because a man and a woman unilaterally and unconditionally promise fidelity to their spouse. The word "if" does not appear at the beginning of your wedding vows. And that means even if your spouse is unfaithful or unable to fulfill her part of the vow, you are still bound. And that might mean celibacy for the rest of your life. That is a sobering thought. But if wedding vows were conditional, all married love would simply be self-love. Authentic love means taking a risk. In this respect, Joseph is the greatest saintly model for every married man. He understood the struggles of being celibate and married, and he became a perfect model of selfless, married love.

Saint Joseph's selfless love is also shown in the great sacrifices he makes for the Christ Child, even though he knows that Child is not his natural son. He moved to Egypt to protect the baby Jesus, and he labored tirelessly and endured many failures and setbacks to provide for Mary's Son. Saint Joseph adopted Jesus in a way analogous to how the eternal Father adopts each baptized Christian. In this way, Saint Joseph is a model for adoptive fathers and stepfathers who, out of love for their spouse, take their children as their own.

There is another aspect of married life in which Saint Joseph is a great model and intercessor. It is inevitable that there will be serious misunderstandings between spouses at different points of their marriage. And sometimes these misunderstandings are not able to be cleared up. The same thing happened in the Holy Family. Joseph could not understand why his wife was pregnant without his cooperation. And there was no way to clear that up without God's help. Mary could not understand why she had to move to Egypt in the middle of the night without so much as saying goodbye to her family. Nor was there any way for Joseph to explain his decision to her. Joseph and Mary could not understand why Jesus had stayed behind in Jerusalem without telling them, leaving them to search three days in sorrow. Yet in all these misunderstandings, love triumphed over the desire to understand. There will be aspects of every man's marriage which he simply will never understand in this life, and in those times, Saint Joseph stands as a model and a compassionate intercessor.

Saint Joseph is also an exemplar and intercessor for priests and consecrated religious men. Every man, even if he has taken a vow of celibacy, has the natural inclination to marriage and begetting children. And as celibate men, we often must interact with women, sometimes women to whom we feel attracted, for the sake of their spiritual needs. Saint Joseph teaches us by his example how to love a woman in utter chastity and purity. He teaches us how to elevate our natural desires and conform them to our supernatural vocation. Saint Joseph, in his own person and vocation, demonstrates that the celibate life is not unnatural or contrary to nature but rather a supernatural way of fulfilling our natural inclinations. Grace builds upon and perfects nature, and Saint Joseph stands as a witness to the perfect harmony which can exist between our natural desires and our supernatural vocation.

Finally, Saint Joseph is a model for single men who are still discerning their vocation. When a young man is searching to know God's will, he is simultaneously striving to achieve self-mastery over his unruly sexual desires and to hear God's voice concerning his vocation. During this time, which is often marked by profound struggle and doubts, discouragement can be a great temptation. Saint Joseph knew doubt and the temptation to discouragement. Having decided to remain celibate, he probably thought he would never find a spouse—something which certainly would have opened him up to ridicule and suspicion in his time and culture. And when, by a miracle of God's providence, he discovered that Mary too wanted to live a virginal marriage, he was confronted with another setback: he discovered that Mary was pregnant without his help. This discovery prompted him to wrestle interiorly with doubts about his own worthiness to live out his vocation, and he even contemplated giving up by quietly divorcing his wife. Yet, through all this, the ears of his heart remained open to God's voice. He did not let discouragement or the battle against his lower nature overcome him, but he trusted completely in God's mercy to accomplish what he realized he could not do by his own abilities. In all this, Saint Joseph serves as a model and also an intercessor who has compassion upon young men who are wrestling with their own interior doubts and temptations to give up.

In sum, Saint Joseph is the perfect model for all men, regardless of their state of life; in his unique vocation, he mysteriously lived out the vocation of every man in a manner which allowed him to be a guide and an understanding intercessor for each of us.

Chapter 7

Protector of the Universal Church

One of the principal theological conclusions to which we can argue using typology is the fact that Saint Joseph is the protector or patron of the whole Church. Blessed Pope Pius IX explicitly used this method when he taught that Saint Joseph is the patron of the universal Church: "As almighty God appointed Joseph, son of the patriarch Jacob, over all the land of Egypt to save grain for the people, so when the fullness of time had come, and he was about to send forth his only-begotten Son, the Savior of the world, he chose another Joseph, of whom the first had been the type, and he made him the lord and chief of his household and possessions, the guardians of his choicest treasures."[41]

Pope Leo XIII argued similarly concerning the same matter:

> The first Joseph won the favor and especial goodwill of his master, and that through Joseph's administration his household came to prosperity and wealth; that (still more important) he presided over the kingdom with great power, and, in a time when the harvests

[41] Pope Pius IX, *Quemadmodum Deus* (Dec. 8, 1870).

> failed, he provided for all the needs of the Egyptians with so much wisdom that the King decreed to him the title "Savior of the world." Thus it is that We may prefigure the new in the old patriarch. And as the first caused the prosperity of his master's domestic interests and at the same time rendered great services to the whole kingdom, so the second, destined to be the guardian of the Christian religion, should be regarded as the protector and defender of the Church, which is truly the house of the Lord and the kingdom of God on earth.[42]

Several Scripture texts form the basis for this typological argument. The primary text concerning the universal authority Joseph the patriarch exercised over the land of Egypt is found in the forty-first chapter of Genesis:

> Pharaoh said to Joseph, "Since God has shown you all this, there is none so discreet and wise as you are; you shall be over my house, and all my people shall order themselves as you command; only as regards the throne will I be greater than you." And Pharaoh said to Joseph, "Behold, I have set you over all the land of Egypt." Then Pharaoh took his signet ring from his hand and put it on Joseph's hand, and arrayed him in garments of fine linen, and put a gold chain about his neck; and he made him to ride in his second chariot; and they cried before him, "Bow the knee!" Thus he set him over all the land of Egypt. Moreover Pharaoh

[42] Pope Leo XIII, *Quamquam Pluries*, no. 4.

> said to Joseph, "I am Pharaoh, and without your consent no man shall lift up hand or foot in all the land of Egypt." (Gn 41:39–44)

To this text we can add two others from the Psalms: "Give ear, O Shepherd of Israel, you who lead Joseph like a flock!" (Ps 80:1); and "He made [Joseph] lord of his house, and ruler of all his possessions, to instruct his princes at his pleasure, and to teach his elders wisdom" (Ps 105:21–22).

The Genesis text shows that Pharaoh gave Joseph universal authority over the land of Egypt. It may seem easy to argue from the fact that Joseph the patriarch is a type of Saint Joseph to the fact that Saint Joseph is patron of the universal Church. However, two significant difficulties must be addressed if we use that reasoning. First, it implies that Pharaoh is a type of God; second, it implies that Egypt is a type of the Church or the Kingdom of God.

How could Pharaoh be a type of God? After all, in the book of Exodus, Pharaoh was a type of the devil! The truth is that some pharaohs were good and beneficent towards the saints, while others tried to harm them. This pharaoh's beneficent and supreme authority in the kingdom shows that he was an apt type of God similar to King Ahasuerus in the book of Esther.

The second difficulty involves Egypt being a type of the Church. After all, Egypt is usually depicted as the enemy of Israel, for they enslaved God's elect. The solution to this difficulty is that Egypt can sometimes be a type for the world inasmuch as it is at war with the Church, but sometimes it refers to the world inasmuch as it is the place where the

Church militant is active and lives. In the present case, Egypt is depicted as a haven for the chosen people as they fled from famine. The chosen people who comprised the Church were welcomed into Egypt and given preferential treatment. Something similar might have been said of the Roman Empire after the conversion of Constantine: the Church was welcomed and not only spared from persecution but even promoted. And so the Egypt of Joseph's time signifies a period when the spiritual and temporal orders are harmonious. Therefore, Egypt in Joseph's day could be a type which includes the Church.

If these two realities are understood, then it implies that Saint Joseph is given universal jurisdiction over the whole Church, and in some way over the whole world, inasmuch as the world is not hostile to the Church. This reading is confirmed by Psalm 80 which refers to Israel as the "flock of Joseph." Israel is a type of the Church, so calling it the flock of Joseph implies that Joseph is a shepherd over the whole Church.

Psalm 105 adds the nuance that not only was Joseph placed over the "house" and "possessions" of God (i.e., the Church and God's holy ones) but also he is entrusted to teach the leaders of God's people wisdom. This implies that Saint Joseph is a special patron for priests and bishops who are seeking divine wisdom.

Let us return to the most detailed passage about the Old Testament Joseph's universal authority (Gn 41). The extensive authority granted by Pharaoh to Joseph is striking. First, he says, "You shall be over my house, and all my people shall order themselves as you command; only as regards the throne will I be greater than you." Joseph is not merely a benevolent patron of those in need. Joseph is in charge. The whole order of the house of Pharaoh and his people is determined by Joseph. So, too, Saint Joseph is not merely a patron and protector of the Church, the house of God. He is in charge. He sets in order and establishes the relationships among the members of the mystical body of Christ. This implies that Saint Joseph is a kind of mediator and distributor of God's graces, since it is in virtue of these graces that persons are ordered within the Church. At Joseph's command, goods are distributed and hierarchical relationships established within the Church. Only as regards the throne—that is, the throne at the right hand of the Father given to Jesus in virtue of the hypostatic union—is Christ greater than Joseph. Yes, the Queen, the Blessed Virgin, sits on Christ's right while Joseph on His left. This implies that all graces (save those given to Jesus and Mary) are distributed by Joseph, not just some. Since Saint Joseph exercised authority over Jesus and Mary while on earth, we ought to be convinced that his authority in heaven is universal.

Next, Pharaoh says to Joseph, "Behold, I have set you over all the land of Egypt." The passage further declares, "Then Pharaoh took his signet ring from his hand and put it on Joseph's hand, and arrayed him in garments of fine linen, and put a gold chain about his neck; and he made him to ride in his second chariot; and they cried before him, 'Bow the knee!' Thus he set him over all the land of Egypt." This passage also signifies Saint Joseph's heavenly glory. Five gifts are conferred upon him: (1) a signet ring, (2) garments of fine linen, (3) a gold chain about his neck, (4) the honor of riding in the second chariot, and (5) the honor of having all the people compelled to bow the knee. The signet ring signifies that Saint Joseph participates in God's very authority. For it was with his signet ring that the king would seal his official edicts which had the force of law (cf. 1 Kgs 21:8). The fine linen garments signify that he was adorned with every virtue and righteous deed: "The linen represents the righteous deeds of the holy ones" (Rv 19:8). The gold chain signifies the wisdom of Saint Joseph, as the book of Sirach implies: "To a sensible man education is like a golden ornament" (Sir 21:21). A gold chain was also conferred upon Daniel for the same reason (see Dn 5:29). Riding in the second chariot signifies that Joseph is second in command in battle. For it was with his chariot that the king went out to confront his enemies, and the second chariot was used by the second in command. The reality that all should bow their knee to Joseph indicates that he shares in the very glory of Christ. For to Christ is due the honor that "at the name of Jesus every knee should bend" (Phil 2:10).

Finally, Pharaoh says to Joseph, "Without your consent no man shall lift up hand or foot in all the land of Egypt." This passage is remarkable in its application to Saint Joseph. For Pharaoh is asserting that Joseph has such universal authority that even their least actions are subject to his consent. Applied to Saint Joseph, this implies that even the least good work (signified by lifting the hand) or the least progress in the spiritual life (signified by lifting the foot) is due to Joseph's consent. Joseph, with Mary, seems to be a universal mediator of divine grace. Whatever graces come from Christ flow through Mary then through Joseph to the rest of the Church. In other words, Saint Joseph "adds" or opens the storehouse of graces like Joseph the patriarch, who distributed seven years' worth of collected food during the famine (see Gn 41:49). Yes, Saint Joseph is the man who was closest to not only Christ but Mary. And therefore, Saint Joseph holds the key to unlocking all the graces that pour forth from the Sacred Heart of Jesus and the Immaculate Heart of Mary. Graces that far exceed the sands on the shore or the stars in heaven.

Theological Arguments That Saint Joseph Is Protector of the Church

Now that we have seen, by way of typology, evidence that Saint Joseph is the protector of the whole Church (and even a universal mediator of the grace of Christ), and that this interpretation has been endorsed by the magisterium of the Church, is it possible to establish this fact with certitude by way of a properly theological argument? At least two arguments can be used to establish definitively that Saint Joseph is the protector of the universal Church. The first argument proceeds from the reality that Saint Joseph was the guardian of the Blessed Virgin Mary. The second relies upon the fact that Saint Joseph was the guardian of the Christ Child. These arguments can be summarized as follows.

The first argument states that Mary was placed by God under Joseph's care and guardianship during her earthly life. But if someone is faithful in carrying out his mission in this life, the authority given to that person in heaven is greater than, yet proportional to, his responsibilities in this life. Therefore, in the life to come, Saint Joseph has authority greater than, yet proportional to, his responsibility of caring for and guarding the Blessed Virgin Mary in this world. Thus, in heaven, Saint Joseph is placed over something greater than Mary, yet proportional to her—namely, the whole Church—for Mary is an image of the Church, and as Saint Augustine says, the Church is greater than Mary.

The second argument is similar but uses a different middle term. In this world, the body of Jesus was placed by God under Saint Joseph's care and guardianship. But if someone is faithful in carrying out his mission in this life, the authority given to that person in the life to come is greater than, yet proportional to, his responsibilities in this life. Therefore, in the life to come, Saint Joseph has authority greater than, yet proportional to, his responsibility of caring for and guarding the body of Jesus in this world. Thus, in heaven, Saint Joseph is placed over something greater than the body of Jesus, yet proportional to it. But what could possibly be greater than the body of Jesus? Saint Paul tells us that it is the Church which is Christ "come to full stature" (Eph 4:13). Therefore, the full Christ, the Church, is placed under the care and guardianship of Saint Joseph.[43]

Both these arguments rely upon the truth that if someone is faithful in carrying out his mission in this life, the

[43] Pope Saint Paul VI makes a version of this argument in a homily on Saint Joseph, saying, "The Church invokes Saint Joseph as her Patron and Protector through her unshakable trust that he to whom Christ willed to confide the care and protection of his own frail human childhood, will continue from heaven to perform his protective task in order to guide and defend the Mystical Body of Christ himself, which is always weak, always under attack, always in a state of peril." Homily on the Solemnity of Saint Joseph, March 19, 1969.

authority which God gives to that person in the life to come is greater than, yet proportional to, his responsibilities in this life. Where do we find this truth revealed in Sacred Scripture? We find this truth revealed in a parable of Jesus recorded in Saint Luke's Gospel. Here is the passage:

> A nobleman went into a far country to receive a kingdom and then return. Calling ten of his servants, he gave them ten pounds, and said to them: "Trade with these till I come." But his citizens hated him and sent an embassy after him, saying: "We do not want this man to reign over us." When he returned, having received the kingdom, he commanded these servants, to whom he had given the money, to be called to him, that he might know what they had gained by trading. The first came before him, saying: "Lord, your pound has made ten pounds more." And he said to him: "Well done, good servant! Because you have been faithful in a very little, you shall have authority over ten cities." And the second came, saying: "Lord, your pound has made five pounds." And he said to him: "And you are to be over five cities." (Lk 19:12–19)

Like all Jesus's parables, this parable requires some interpretation. There are many questions we could ask about this parable. For example, who is the nobleman? Who are the servants? What is the far country and the kingdom? What does the return of the nobleman signify? But the central question which needs to be answered for our purposes is: Why is the reward for trading with the nobleman's money governorship over a proportionate number of cities?

It is clear that the nobleman in this parable signifies Jesus. Jesus is noble because of His human birth in time—He is a son of David the king (as the genealogies of both Matthew and Luke attest). Jesus is also noble due to His divine birth from all eternity (cf. Heb 1:5). This double nobility of Jesus is clearly stated by the angel Gabriel during the Annunciation: "He will be great and will be called Son of the Most High, and the Lord God will give him the throne of David his father" (Lk 1:32). The parable's other details confirm this reality. The servants are those who profess faith in Jesus and follow Him as His disciples. The far country is the next life, for it was after His death that Christ was crowned king, as Saint Paul states: "He humbled himself, becoming obedient to death, even death on a cross. Because of this, God greatly exalted him and bestowed on him the name that is above every name" (Phil 2:8–9). The return of the nobleman signifies the return of Jesus at the end of time when He shall judge each man and reward him according to his deeds (see Acts 10:42).

This leads us to the answer to the final question: Why is governorship over a certain number of cities the reward for trading with the nobleman's money? The first thing to notice is that the number of cities over which each is granted authority is the same as the number of talents which they returned to their master. This means that there is a *proportion* between our labors in this life and our reward in the next. This proportion is the reason Saint Peter exhorts the faithful to "rejoice in the same proportion that you share Christ's sufferings, that you may also rejoice and be glad when his glory is revealed" (1 Pt 4:13). Yet there is a very wide distance between the value of a talent and the value of a city. This implies that the reward, while proportional to our labors in one sense, is vastly disproportionate in another sense, as Saint Paul teaches in many places: "The sufferings of this present time are as nothing compared with the glory to be revealed for us" (Rom 8:18); and again, "this momentary light affliction is producing for us an eternal weight of glory beyond all comparison," (2 Cor 4:17). So Jesus gives His servants authority over small matters in this life, but when He returns, He gives those who were successful authority over much greater matters in the next life: "Since you were faithful in small matters, I will give you great responsibilities" (Mt 25:12).

This parable reminds us that if we are faithful in carrying out our mission in this life, the authority which God gives to us in the life to come is greater than, yet proportional to, our responsibilities in this life. This was the very premise by which we demonstrated that Saint Joseph has been given authority over the whole Church by God as a reward for being faithful in the "small matters" of caring for Mary and Jesus.

What Does It Mean to Say That Joseph Is Patron of the Church?

After arguing through typology and from the plain sense of Scripture that Saint Joseph is the patron of the Universal Church, we are in a better position to reflect upon what it means to say that Saint Joseph is the patron of the Universal Church. First, it means that Saint Joseph protects the Church from her enemies—namely, the demons and those men who are used as their instruments for attacking the Church. The Litany of Saint Joseph recognizes Saint Joseph's powerful patronage when it invokes him as "terror of demons."

Second, being patron of the whole Church means that Saint Joseph establishes the order among the members of the Church, just as the governor of a city establishes the order among its citizens. And since the order among the citizens of the Church is determined by the mutual relationships among its members, and because these relationships are determined by the knowledge and grace communicated from one member of the Church to another, this implies that Saint Joseph is responsible for distributing divine truth and grace to each Catholic. Ordinarily, this is accomplished through the sacramental hierarchy of the Church. Referring to this, Saint Paul teaches that Christ "gave some as apostles, others as prophets, others as evangelists, others as pastors and teachers, to equip the holy ones for the work of ministry, for building up the body of Christ" (Eph 4:11–12). But God sometimes confers these gifts of truth and grace by means of certain charismatic gifts as well. In another place, Saint Paul provides a more exhaustive list: "Now you are Christ's body, and individually parts of it. Some people God has designated in the church to be, first, apostles; second, prophets; third, teachers; then, mighty deeds; then, gifts of healing, assistance, administration, and varieties of tongues" (1 Cor 12:27–28). Thus, Saint Joseph is a kind of universal distributor of God's manifold grace. Jesus seems to refer to this when He said: "Who, then, is the faithful and prudent servant, whom the master has put in charge of his household to distribute to them their food at the proper time?" (Mt 24:45).

Third, the fact that Saint Joseph is the patron of the Universal Church implies that he guides the direction of the Church through time until the day of salvation, just as a shepherd guides his flock until they are safely home.

Finally, Saint Joseph's authority as patron of the Universal Church implies that he provides for the spiritual and temporal needs of the Church, just as a shepherd provides for the needs of his flock by providing them with water and copious green fields: "He makes me lie down in green pastures. He leads me beside still waters" (Ps 23:2).

Devotion to Saint Joseph, Patron of the Universal Church

Devotion to a particular saint matures and is strengthened when we understand better the place of that saint within God's overall salvific plan. In the case of Saint Joseph, the first thing which strikes us is his universal influence. His patronage is not limited to this or that particular area of need, which indicates his supreme influence over the entire heavenly court. And just as those who are higher in authority are due greater honor, so too is Saint Joseph due the highest veneration among the saints alongside Mary. After Our Lady, God wills us to honor Saint Joseph most of all.

Because Saint Joseph is our protector against the Church's foes, he should be invoked against the assaults of demons and of evil men who are attempting to destroy our faith in Christ and His Church. When a young woman is being attacked by demons of despair or a young man is experiencing assaults by demons of lust, Saint Joseph will be there to drive them away. When the enemies of the Church (either local or universal) seem too powerful to resist, and when no human hope is left, we must turn to Saint Joseph.

As guardian of the Church, Saint Joseph governs and establishes the order among the members of the Church, as indicated by the passage "without your consent no man shall lift up hand or foot in all the land" (Gn 41:44). As such, he has tremendous influence over relationships among members of the Church. When family relationships, such as marriage or between parents and children, are breaking down, Saint Joseph can aid us in the most powerful way. He knew how great the strains can be on family relationships. He experienced extremely difficult family situations, such as finding out that his wife was pregnant without his cooperation, and living without work in a foreign land. He also endured the stress of losing the child Jesus for three days. Even when there was no way to understand how or why his wife and child were behaving, Joseph exercised that love which believes all things (1 Cor 13:7). Therefore, Saint Joseph is supremely compassionate towards those who are experiencing trying family situations. Saint Joseph also governs the Church's overall structure. When the hierarchy fails in its obligations to teach and sanctify God's people, Saint Joseph can influence the order among bishops, priests, and deacons, as well as the religious and laity, so that we come to no harm due to the shortcomings of those from whom we have a right to expect wisdom and holiness.

Because Saint Joseph guides the Church throughout history until the day of salvation, he is able to obtain for us the grace of trusting completely in God's providence. During his lifetime, Saint Joseph had to live a life of complete trust in God's guiding hand. When he often experienced failure and uncertainty, Saint Joseph did not permit his fears to overcome or even discourage him; rather, he trusted completely in God's hidden plan. He is able to obtain for us the same grace which he merited to receive.

Finally, because Saint Joseph provides for the Church's spiritual and temporal needs, we can turn to him as a loving father for everything. So often young people today are deprived of a father, either through divorce, abandonment, or some other cause. I send all of these young people to Saint Joseph. In him they find a loving father who listens to their needs and fills their hearts with sound spiritual counsel. So often, many people find themselves in dire financial straits. They fear losing their job, their home, and their health. Saint Joseph knew suffering, especially these anxieties. He endured the humiliation of being able to provide only a cave, a stable for animals, as the birthplace for Jesus. He fled to Egypt where he did not know the language, where he had no work or family to support him. And his life was probably shortened significantly because of the many long working hours and sacrifices required to support Jesus and Mary. By the world's standards, Saint Joseph was a financial failure, yet he was the best human father who ever lived, the most perfect icon of God the Father our race has begotten. Because of his personal experience with failure and disappointment, Saint Joseph is especially compassionate to those facing great poverty. In fact, one of his great titles in the Litany of Saint Joseph is "lover of poverty." We can entrust all of our temporal needs to him.

Chapter 8

Guardian and Provider of the Eucharist

At this point, it is important to look back at the overall story of Joseph's ascent to power in the kingdom of Egypt in order to understand more fully the implications of Saint Joseph's universal authority over the Church. Recall that the reason Joseph the patriarch was elevated to the place second after Pharaoh was because he was able to accurately interpret the dream of Pharaoh about the seven years of plenty and the seven years of famine. Moreover, he wisely counseled that during the seven years of plenty, a ration of the crops be saved in granaries to be distributed during the years of famine. Thus, Pharaoh placed him over all the land and gave him authority to ration and distribute grain to the people. If the universal authority granted to Joseph the patriarch was a type of the universal authority of Saint Joseph over the Church, then the obvious question to ask is: What does Joseph's role in distributing grain to all the world typify? Grain, of course, is the matter from which bread is made. And in the New Testament, the most important fulfillment of bread as a type is the Eucharist. It makes sense intuitively that if Saint Joseph is the guardian of the universal Church, which is the mystical body of Christ, then Saint Joseph would also be the guardian over the sacramental body of Christ, the most holy Eucharist. Perhaps this is what is signified when we read in Saint Matthew's Gospel that Saint Joseph watched over Jesus when He was born in Bethlehem, which means "house of bread." Later on, we shall formulate a theological argument which establishes this connection, but for now, it is enough to see the fittingness of Saint Joseph's role as guardian and provider of the Eucharist.

The Argument From Typology

The central text which, as a type, shows that Saint Joseph is the guardian and provider of the Eucharist, is the text in which the distribution of grain to the whole world is entrusted to the authority of Joseph the patriarch: "When the famine had spread over all the land, Joseph opened all the storehouses, and sold to the Egyptians, for the famine was severe in the land of Egypt. Moreover, all the earth came to Egypt to Joseph to buy grain, because the famine was severe over all the earth" (Gn 41:56–57).

If Joseph the patriarch was the one from whom not only the Egyptians but even the whole world had to obtain bread to live upon, the obvious typological significance for Saint Joseph is that the whole world in some way needs to go to Joseph to obtain the Bread of Life, the Eucharist.

But it is worthwhile here to ask the question: What does it mean to say that Saint Joseph is guardian and provider of the Eucharist? After all, it seems that every priest, without Saint Joseph's help, can provide the Eucharist to whomever he wishes and that every priest is somehow a guardian of the Eucharist. To say that Saint Joseph is a guardian and provider of the Eucharist is simply to recognize that before any priest is enabled to consecrate or distribute the Eucharist, Saint Joseph must somehow give his approval, just as Joseph the patriarch had to give his approval before any grain was distributed to the people. Saint Joseph is mysteriously involved whenever the Body of Jesus is given; since he had care over that body in its natural form on earth, he continues to exercise care over that body in its sacramental form from heaven.

And just as there is a definite relationship between the governing authority of Joseph the patriarch over Egypt and his authority in distributing grain, so too there is a similar relationship between Saint Joseph's authority over the universal Church and his provision over the Eucharist. The primary reason Joseph was placed over Egypt was because he had, as a gift from God, the foresight to preserve the grain in times of famine. So also God gave Saint Joseph the foresight to protect and preserve the body of the Child Jesus, lest the world be deprived of the Bread of Life. As a heavenly reward, God has placed Saint Joseph over the sacramental body of Jesus in order to provide this living Bread to all who need it and who are willing to pay the appropriate price.

Recent events have manifested that the distribution of the Eucharist is not simply something the faithful can take for granted. For several months beginning in Lent of 2020 until after Easter that year, most of the Church, indeed the whole world, was deprived of the Bread of Life. As I reread Genesis 47, I was struck by its apparent fulfillment today:

When the money was all spent in the land of Egypt and in the land of Canaan, all the Egyptians came to Joseph, and said, "Give us food; why should we die before your eyes? For our money is gone." And Joseph answered, "Give your cattle, and I will give you food in exchange for your cattle, if your money is gone." So they brought their cattle to Joseph; and Joseph gave them food in exchange for the horses, the flocks, the herds, and the asses: and he supplied them with food in exchange for all their cattle that year. And when that year was ended, they came to him the following year, and said to him, "We will not hide from my lord that our money is all spent; and the herds of cattle are my lord's; there is nothing left in the sight of my lord but our bodies and our lands. Why should we die before your eyes, both we and our land? Buy us and our land for food, and we with our land will be slaves to Pharaoh; and give us seed, that we may live, and not die, and that the land may not be desolate." So Joseph bought all the land of Egypt for Pharaoh; for all the Egyptians sold their fields, because the famine was severe upon them. The land became Pharaoh's; and as for the people, he made slaves of them from one end of Egypt to the other. Only the land of the priests he did not buy; for the priests had a fixed allowance from Pharaoh, and lived on the allowance which Pharaoh gave them; therefore they did not sell their land. (Gn 47:15–22)

As the famine progressed, the people sought Joseph's help many times, each time offering more in order to receive grain to live. First, they gave all their money, then their livestock, then their fields and their own bodies so that they became Pharaoh's slaves. Interestingly, only the priests were exempt from this since they already received regular support from Pharaoh. In what seems to be a strange, prophetic fulfillment of Genesis 47, for the most part, it was the priests and religious who had regular access to the Eucharist during those dark months of 2020. Even most of those religious houses which could not have Mass regularly at least had communion services because an excess of hosts had been consecrated for them. In times of Eucharistic famine, it seems as if Saint Joseph will provide the Eucharist to those who give their property, bodies, and even freedom to God through religious profession. But the priests will always have their provision of the Eucharist through the power of their ordination.

Theological Demonstration

Even though the likenesses between Genesis 47 and today is fascinating, Saint Joseph's certain authority over the Eucharist is the real focus. Given our understanding of scriptural types, can we also come to the same conclusion using the New Testament?

Yes, a sound theological argument can be made based on a few clear texts. Here is the argument in outline:

Saint Joseph had care of Christ's physical body. But one who has care over Christ's physical body ought also to have care over His sacramental body. Therefore, Saint Joseph has care over the sacramental Body of Christ—namely, the most holy Eucharist.

The first premise is obvious in Scripture. The angel commanded Joseph in a dream to protect the child Jesus from Herod: "An angel of the Lord appeared to Joseph in a dream and said, 'Rise, take the child and his mother, and flee to Egypt, and remain there till I tell you; for Herod is about to search for the child, to destroy him.' And he rose and took the child and his mother by night, and departed to Egypt" (Mt 2:13–14).

The angel gave these instructions to Joseph because the well-being of the child was in Joseph's charge. Therefore, the angel did not take the child himself, nor did he instruct Mary to take the child.

The second premise is that "one who has care over Christ's physical body ought also to have care over His sacramental body." While this premise seems intuitively correct, it needs some clarification and defense. For example, there are many differences between Christ's physical body and His sacramental body. Perhaps these differences are one reason Saint Joseph has authority over one and not the other. Also, Saint Joseph's authority over Christ's body seems to have ended when Christ became a man, for then Christ would have governed His own body in a way that was not subject to Saint Joseph. But now that Christ is a man and reigns in heaven, it seems unfitting that another should have care over His sacramental body.

To understand the truth of the latter statement, we must realize that Christ's sacramental body is the very same body which Saint Joseph cared for: the only difference between the two is that Christ's sacramental body is hidden under the outward appearances of bread and wine, while Saint Joseph cared for that body while it existed with its own proper outward appearance. While Christ was wrapped in swaddling clothes, and His body was mostly hidden from view, Saint Joseph still cared for that part of Christ's body which lay hidden. So also now that the whole substance of Christ's body is hidden, there is no reason Saint Joseph should not have care over that very body.

Now someone might object and say: "But there is no need to guard Christ's sacramental body from harm, since one who does physical harm to Christ's sacramental body does not harm Jesus's physical body." Had Herod cut a consecrated host in two, the Christ Child would have slept soundly through it all. In response to this objection, we must realize that a father cares not only for the physical well-being of his child but even for his good reputation and honor. It is difficult to imagine a good father standing by silently when someone is slandering his son or spitting upon his son. So Saint Joseph's care for Christ's body extends also to the honor due that body, and it is in this way that Saint Joseph continues to be a guardian of Christ's sacramental body.

What should we say to the second objection; namely, now that Jesus is a man, there is no need for Joseph to be involved? It is true that once a man comes of age, he cares for the good of his own body. But it does not follow from this that his father no longer has any care for his son's body. Why does a father confer an inheritance upon his son if not to somehow continue to provide for the needs of his body? Indeed, the father of the prodigal son did just this, and even when his son returned home emaciated and all covered with tatters, the first thing that merciful father did was provide for the needs of his son's body with a robe, shoes, and a banquet. So also, Saint Joseph continues to care for the body of his son Jesus.

Another way to see the truth of the statement that one who has care of Jesus's physical body has care over His sacramental body is to see it as a particular application of the principle that one who has care of the greater has care of the lesser contained by that greater. For example, if someone has care over the family, he has care over each member of that family. Or if someone is in charge of teaching grammar to his students, then he also is in charge of teaching nouns and verbs since these are contained under grammar. Again, if someone has care of a child, he has care of that same child when he is both at home and away from home, since he is the same child whether he is at home or away from home. Caring for a child when he is away from home is simply part of caring for that child. But Jesus's sacramental body is simply an extension of His natural body now present in a different manner. Therefore, caring for Jesus's body includes caring for that same body under its sacramental form.

Saint Thomas Aquinas uses a similar statement in arguing that a priest has authority in the Church. He argues from the link between the Eucharist and the mystical body of Christ to establish the fact that priests exercise authority over the Church because they exercise authority over the Eucharist:

> The power which a priest has over the mystical body depends upon the power which he has over the true body of Christ.[44]
>
> Since sacramental grace descends into the mystical body from the head, it follows that every sacramental operation in the mystical body, through which grace is given, depends upon the sacramental operation over the true body of the Lord. And therefore, only the priest is able to absolve in the penitential forum and baptize in virtue of his office.[45]

Saint Thomas argues here that a priest has care for the mystical body of Christ, the Church, because he has care of the sacramental body of Christ, the Eucharist. For an even stronger reason, then, it is clear that one who has care over the physical body of Christ has care over His sacramental body. Besides, we have already seen that Saint Joseph has care over the mystical body of Christ in a way superior to any priest, since Saint Joseph's authority is universal. We can now see more clearly that Saint Joseph has care over Christ's sacramental body, and this is the middle term connecting His authority over Christ's physical body and the mystical body of Christ! Saint Joseph is the patron of the universal Church precisely because he is the guardian of the Eucharist!

---

[44] *Commentary on the Fourth Book of the Sentences of Peter Lombard,* d.18, q.1, a.1c.

[45] *Commentary on the Fourth Book of the Sentences of Peter Lombard,* d.7, q.3, a.1c.

Another Gospel passage that deserves our attention pertains to Saint Joseph's authority over the Eucharistic body of Christ. Found in Saint Matthew's Gospel, here is the passage in context:

> Watch therefore, for you do not know on what day your Lord is coming. But know this, that if the householder had known in what part of the night the thief was coming, he would have watched and would not have let his house be broken into. Therefore you also must be ready; for the Son of man is coming at an hour you do not expect. *Who then is the faithful and wise servant, whom his Master has set over his household, to give them their food at the proper time? Blessed is that servant whom his Master when he comes will find so doing. Truly, I say to you, he will set him over all his possessions.* (Mt 24:42–47)

If we were to hear Jesus ask this simple question in isolation: "Who is the faithful and wise servant whom God has set over his household?" The most obvious answer would be Saint Joseph.[46] Saint Joseph was the only servant placed over the actual household of the Master—namely, the household of Jesus. And just in case you overlooked this reality, Jesus goes on to add "to give them their food at the proper time" and adds that his reward will be that "he will set him over all his possessions." Now in the Scriptures, is there anyone who was deputed to give out food at the

[46] In fact, the Church in her liturgy sanctions just this interpretation. In the votive Mass for Saint Joseph, this Scripture passage is quoted nearly verbatim and applied to him.

proper time and who received as his reward being put over the master's possessions? The answer is, clearly and unambiguously, Joseph the patriarch. So in this passage, Jesus is clearly linking His father Joseph with Joseph the patriarch and asserting that His father Joseph would receive a mission and a reward like that of Joseph the patriarch. Read in its plain, literal sense, the most obvious sense of this passage is that God set Saint Joseph over His household and that he provided Jesus and Mary with their daily sustenance. This passage is luminously clear when it is taken to refer to Saint Joseph's role in providing for the Holy Family. Not only that, but when we look at the larger implications of Saint Joseph's role not only as the head of the Holy Family but also over the household of God which is the Church, we see that Saint Joseph was entrusted with providing for the spiritual sustenance of the whole Church. And what is the primary food for the whole Church? The Holy Eucharist!

Now to be fair, the overall context of the passage refers to being ready for the second coming of Jesus. And as the passage continues, it also speaks about the punishment for those who might fail in their duty (which could not be said about Saint Joseph). So the passage in context can be applied to anyone who is a steward set over God's household. While the passage has a broader application beyond Saint Joseph, it can still refer to him especially or even primarily. Many Scripture passages refer to multiple persons or things yet have one primary referent in mind. For example, the passage from Hosea: "Out of Egypt I have called my son" (Hos 11:1) can be taken to refer to many realities. This passage refers to the whole people of Israel but has a special prophetic application to Jesus Himself, who is primarily the Son of God.[47] Similarly, the passage about the faithful and wise servant can also refer to those placed in some way over the household of God, but it is especially and primarily fulfilled in Saint Joseph.

By examining the context of this passage, we can reach another insightful conclusion. Because Jesus refers to His second coming like a thief, He beckons us to be vigilant. Then He immediately raises the question of who is that faithful and prudent steward. It is telling that He asks this as a question, as if He wants us to reflect upon who it could be. As stated earlier, perhaps that steward is each Christian who cares for others or is placed over others. And yet, the likenesses to Saint Joseph are so pronounced that one cannot help but think that Jesus also had Saint Joseph in mind. So, given the context, who is this steward who is crucial at the moment of the Lord's coming? If He refers to His coming at each person's death, this seems to be a reference to the crucial role Saint Joseph plays at the death of each Christian as the patron of a happy death. If it refers to His coming at the end of the world, this seems to apply to Saint Joseph's role in the end times in ushering the Church into eternity.

Devotion to Saint Joseph, Guardian and Provider of the Eucharist

When we reflect upon Saint Joseph's role in caring for and providing the Eucharist, we realize that we have a tremendous motive for gratitude to Saint Joseph which we never

[47] See Saint Thomas Aquinas, *Commentary on Matthew*, ch. 2, lect. 4.

before recognized: each and every time we have received Jesus in the Eucharist, Saint Joseph was somehow responsible. How could we ever repay him for so great a gift, much less for a lifetime of such gifts?

Furthermore, the recent Eucharistic famine throughout the world reminds us that we can never take the Holy Eucharist, the gift surpassing all gifts, for granted. We cannot assume that we have a right to the Holy Eucharist, that we can always receive Jesus whenever we choose or desire. And it is possible that a future famine awaits us. God forbid that will occur, but we know whom to seek so that we shall receive our daily bread.

This raises another question: Why doesn't Saint Joseph intercede to ensure that everyone who desires the Eucharist can receive it? Certainly, many souls who desired to receive Communion were denied access to the Eucharist during that difficult time. One reason this happened was because few souls, even worthy ones, thought to ask this gift from Saint Joseph. Moreover, Saint Joseph is not merely a blind distributor of the Eucharist but a prudent one, who not only ensures that Jesus's sacramental body is given to those who are worthy to receive it but also guards and protects the same sacramental body of Jesus from sacrilege or indifference. Perhaps there were many unworthy communions in the years preceding that Eucharistic famine. That famine gave each Catholic an opportunity to reflect on whether they were approaching the Eucharist worthily.

Our devotion to Saint Joseph should grow and expand to include *thanksgiving* for this most sublime gift of the Son of

God Himself, truly present in the most holy Eucharist, and *petition* that we might be given this gift, and more importantly, that we be found worthy in His eyes to receive so great a guest.

Chapter 9

Patron of a Happy Death

For cradle Catholics, the invocation of Saint Joseph, patron of a happy death, is proverbial. It is, perhaps, his most recognized title. Saint Alphonsus de Liguori encouraged everyone to cherish a special devotion to Saint Joseph in order that he might obtain for each the grace of a happy death. Yet, for most Catholics, little thought is given to the scriptural foundations of this attribution. Certainly, there is much by way of anecdotal evidence to persuade us of the fact that Saint Joseph is the patron of a happy death. The late Father Benedict Groeschel liked to tell the story of an Italian Franciscan who had a great devotion to Saint Joseph and asked everyone he met to pray for his happy death. Sure enough, when the time came for him to depart this life, he sat up and joyfully exclaimed "Arrivederci!" and forthwith entered the next life. But the Scriptures offer us a more certain and solid foundation for asserting that Saint Joseph has been entrusted by God with the special care of those who pass from this life to the next.

Before we consider the scriptural foundations of why Saint Joseph can be called the patron of a happy death, we will explore what the expression "happy death" could possibly mean. No doubt, there is a kind of paradox in the phrase "happy death." Death is among the greatest evils man can endure, since it seems that by death every good is taken away from the one who dies. On the contrary, happiness is man's greatest good. So calling a death "happy" sounds like calling an evil "good." To be the patron of a happy death seems to amount to being the patron of a good evil!

This paradox would remain if in fact death were the ultimate evil. But if death is not the ultimate evil, and in fact can even be turned into a means of acquiring great good, the paradox vanishes. Since Jesus came into the world, death no longer holds dominion: "And when this which is corruptible clothes itself with incorruptibility and this which is mortal clothes itself with immortality, then the word that is written shall come about: 'Death is swallowed up in victory. Where, O death, is your victory? Where, O death, is your sting?' The sting of death is sin, and the power of sin is the law. But thanks be to God who gives us the victory through our Lord Jesus Christ" (1 Cor 15:54–57 NABRE).

So death does not hold the final victory. Moreover, God has made death itself an instrument of salvation and the way to life. First of all, Jesus used death to conquer sin and Satan: "Now since the children share in blood and flesh, he likewise shared in them, that through death he might destroy the one who has the power of death, that is, the devil, and free those who through fear of death had been subject to slavery all their life" (Heb 2:14–15 NABRE). Not only did Jesus use death as a means to accomplish His will, but those who follow Christ also make use of death as a means of salvation, since it leads to the resurrection of life: "For if we have grown into union with him through a death like his, we shall also be united with him in the resurrection" (Rom 6:5 NABRE; see Phil 3:11). Saint Ambrose even compares death to a remedy or medicine.[48] And Saint Teresa of Avila was reported to have said, "I want to see God, but to see him I must die." This explains how someone can have a happy death. A happy death is a death filled with hope in the resurrection and the defeat of sin and Satan.

We are now in a better position to return to the scriptural foundations of Saint Joseph's patronage. Although not expressly defined, the reason Saint Joseph is the patron of a happy death is because he died in the arms of Jesus and Mary. Thus, he had the greatest possible consolations during his death. But this consolation was not merely found in the bodily presence of Jesus and Mary at his deathbed, for death would remove him from their physical presence. Rather, it was because Jesus and Mary inspired the liveliest confidence and hope in the resurrection and in the overcoming of sin and Satan that Saint Joseph experienced such a happy death.

Saint Joseph is believed to have died when Jesus was between the ages of twelve and thirty—the latter being the start of Jesus's public ministry. The glaring absence of Saint Joseph in the Gospel accounts of Jesus's adult life is the most obvious reason for deducing that Saint Joseph died before Jesus turned thirty. In the Gospel accounts depicting Jesus's childhood, Joseph was constantly present. On the other hand, Joseph's absence from the Gospel accounts depicting Jesus's adult life is inexplicable unless Saint Joseph was no longer

[48] Saint Ambrose, *Treatise on Death as a Blessing*, CSEL 32.

present in the earthly life of Jesus and Mary. So the fact that Joseph was in the company of Jesus and Mary at his death seems certain, and this is the testimony of many saints.[49]

Father Donald Calloway gives an excellent reason why, in God's providence, Saint Joseph should have been permitted to die before Jesus began His public ministry: "If Saint Joseph were alive during the public ministry of Jesus, it would have been confusing for people to hear Jesus speak about his desire to take them to his Father. In order to avoid obscuring the primacy of the Heavenly Father, Joseph had to die before the public ministry of Jesus began."[50]

But can we conclude from these facts alone that Saint Joseph is the patron of a happy death? After all, to be the patron of a happy death means more than just having experienced a happy death. When we invoke Saint Joseph as the patron of a happy death, we believe that he can and will obtain for us a happy death like his. Yet, the Gospels are very silent on this question, just as Saint Joseph was silent in Scripture. Once again, the first place we can look is typology to see if anything was said about this matter in the life or the types of Saint Joseph.

---

[49] For example, Saint Bernadine of Siena, Saint Peter Julian Eymard, and Blessed Anne Catherine Emmerich all taught that Jesus and Mary were present at the death of Saint Joseph.

[50] Donald Calloway, *Consecration to Saint Joseph: The Wonders of Our Spiritual Father* (Stockbridge, MA: Marian Press, 2020), 207. It seems to me that it is also fitting that Saint Joseph would not have been permitted by God to be present at Jesus's crucifixion. Can you imagine Saint Joseph sitting quietly by as the soldiers crucified his son? I suppose that he would have fought to prevent Jesus from being crucified, and it would have been right for him to do so, but it would have been contrary to God's plan.

Typological Evidence That Saint Joseph Is the Patron of a Happy Death

As mentioned above, Saint Joseph is called the patron of a happy death for two apparent reasons. First, he can be considered the patron of a happy death because he himself experienced the happiest of deaths. Second, (and more importantly) Saint Joseph has the power to obtain for us the grace of a happy death.

The Principal Types of Joseph All Had Happy Deaths

A probable argument from typology that Saint Joseph had a happy death can be found in the fact that each of the clear types of Saint Joseph were graced with a happy death. Concerning Joseph the patriarch we read: "Joseph died at the age of a hundred and ten. He was embalmed and laid to rest in a coffin in Egypt" (Gn 50:26 NABRE). The embalming of Joseph can be taken as a sign of Saint Joseph's incorruptible body after his death, as he awaited the final resurrection. By this verse we can understand that Saint Joseph died in the hope of the future resurrection of the body.

About Abraham it is written: "Abraham breathed his last and died in a good old age, an old man and full of years, and was gathered to his people" (Gn 25:8). Concerning Isaac, it is written: "Now the days of Isaac were a hundred and eighty years. And Isaac breathed his last; and he died and was gathered to his people" (Gn 35:28–29). Finally, the death of Jacob is described in these terms: "When Jacob had finished giving these instructions to his sons, he drew his feet into the bed, breathed his last, and was gathered to his people" (Gn

49:33). Each of these patriarchs died full of years and were gathered to their kindred. And these kindred were among the elect of God. Thus, Jesus Himself stated that Abraham, Isaac, and Jacob were alive in the presence of God: "Concerning the resurrection of the dead, have you not read what was said to you by God, 'I am the God of Abraham, the God of Isaac, and the God of Jacob?' He is not the God of the dead but of the living" (Mt 22:31–32). So according to each of these types, we find evidence that Saint Joseph too awaited the future resurrection in hope and was gathered together with the elect—clearly, a most happy death.

Joseph the Patriarch Is the Reason for Jacob's Happy Death

When we call Saint Joseph the patron of a happy death, we intend to signify that he can obtain for us the grace of a happy death. And we find evidence for this in Scripture. After Joseph the patriarch revealed himself to his brothers, he sent a message to his father, Israel (Jacob), that he should come out of Canaan to Egypt. This request was met with some hesitation by Israel. After all, he was now dwelling in the land which God had promised as an everlasting inheritance to him and his fathers before him. As much as Israel wanted to see Joseph, he seemed to be in doubt whether it was God's will that he should leave the Promised Land for Egypt. At this point, God intervened to reveal to Israel that it was indeed His will that he and his descendants sojourn in Egypt for a time: for the Lord would lead them back to the Promised Land sometime in the future: "And God spoke to

Israel in visions of the night, and said, 'Jacob, Jacob.' And he said, 'Here am I.' Then he said, 'I am God, the God of your father; do not be afraid to go down to Egypt; for I will there make of you a great nation. I will go down with you to Egypt, and I will also bring you up again; and Joseph's hand shall close your eyes'" (Gn 46:2–4).

In this brief revelation, God makes four promises to Jacob. First, he will make of him a great nation. Second, he will go down with Jacob to Egypt. Third, he will bring Jacob up again from Egypt. Fourth, he promises that Joseph's hand shall close his eyes. This fourth promise seems to be an assurance from God that Jacob will be consoled at his death by the presence of Joseph. This is a typological confirmation of the Catholic belief that by his presence at our death, Saint Joseph will be a consolation to us.

But there is something even deeper in this passage. Look again at the third promise: "I will also bring you up again." How will God bring Jacob up again to the Promised Land if Joseph will close his eyes in death while he is in Egypt? In fact, the book of Genesis records that Jacob died in Egypt (see Gn 49:33). So how did the Lord bring Jacob up again from Egypt? The implication is that God brought Jacob from Egypt into the true promised land, heaven. Thus, Joseph is not only a consolation by being present at Jacob's death but also a consolation as a pledge of entrance into eternal life. Joseph closing his eyes to this world is a portent of a happy entrance into heaven.

There is another interesting detail concerning Jacob's death. When Jacob had died, Joseph ordered that his body be embalmed: "Then Joseph fell on his father's face, and wept over him, and kissed him. And Joseph commanded his servants the physicians to embalm his father. So the physicians embalmed Israel" (Gn 50:1–2). The effect of embalming was to prevent corruption of the dead body. One of the prophecies of the resurrection describes it in just these terms: "You shall not allow your faithful one to see corruption" (Ps 16:10 Vulgate). Here again we find typological evidence that Saint Joseph is somehow responsible for obtaining for us the grace of incorruptibility in the resurrection of the body.

So we see that the principal type of Saint Joseph, Joseph the patriarch, was the cause of the happy death of his father. Therefore, he typifies Saint Joseph's ability to procure a happy death for each one of us.

Theological Argument That Saint Joseph Is the Patron of a Happy Death

We can confirm the typological evidence that Saint Joseph is the patron of a happy death by means of arguments taken from the truths revealed about Saint Joseph in the New Testament. It is certain that someone who has received the benefit of a happy death would be, out of sheer gratitude, exceedingly solicitous to obtain that grace for others. Joseph was the only member of the Holy Family who had the consolation of having his entire family present at his death. Both Jesus and Mary were present at the death of Joseph. But Joseph would not be present at the death of Jesus or Mary, as Simeon implied when he spoke only to Mary about the sword piercing her heart: "Simeon blessed them and said to Mary his mother: 'Behold, this child is destined for the fall and rise of many in Israel, and to be a sign that will be contradicted (and you yourself a sword will pierce) so that the thoughts of many hearts may be revealed'" (Lk 2:34–35 NABRE). Having received the great gift of a happy death, Saint Joseph desires the same grace for us. And so, we can conclude that Saint Joseph, in gratitude for this great gift, would be exceedingly solicitous to obtain a happy death for all who ask for that grace through his intercession.

There is also another argument we can construct based upon the truths established in the previous chapter. We have already seen that Saint Joseph has a unique role to play in the sacramental economy insofar as he is a special dispenser and provider of the Eucharist. But it is precisely through the Eucharist that we obtain the gift of incorruptibility in the resurrection. Jesus makes this clear in his great Eucharistic discourse in John 6:

> Truly, truly, I say to you, he who believes has eternal life. I am the bread of life. Your fathers ate the manna in the wilderness, and they died. This is the bread which comes down from heaven, that a man may eat of it and not die. I am the living bread which came down from heaven; if any one eats of this bread, he will live forever; and the bread which I shall give for the life of the world is my flesh. . . . Truly, truly, I say to you, unless you eat the flesh of the Son of man and drink his blood, you have no life in you; he who eats my flesh and drinks my blood has eternal life, and I will raise him up at the last day. For my flesh is food indeed, and my blood is drink indeed. He who eats

> my flesh and drinks my blood abides in me, and I in him. As the living Father sent me, and I live because of the Father, so he who eats me will live because of me. (Jn 6:47–51, 53–57)

In this text, Jesus teaches that the Eucharist is the cause of our resurrection. His argument is that just as He has received life from the Father, whoever receives His body and blood in the Eucharist will receive life from Him. And thus, it is in virtue of the life-giving power of the Eucharist that Jesus will raise us up on the last day.

So if Saint Joseph is the one who is entrusted by God with the office of providing the Eucharist to us (just as Joseph was entrusted by Pharaoh with the office of providing grain for the whole world), and the Eucharist causes the incorruptible life of the resurrection, it follows that Saint Joseph is somehow responsible for our hope in the resurrection and our happy death.

Devotion to Saint Joseph, Patron of a Happy Death

Everyone desires a happy death, so devotion to Saint Joseph under this special patronage seems as if it would be only natural and easy. But the truth is that many, if not most, people spend their time avoiding the thought of death. Instead, they distract themselves with countless passing things, such as the internet or social media. So many people act as if they will never die, deceiving themselves until the very end.

This kind of life is contrary to the counsel of Sacred Scripture which states: "Remember your last days, set enmity aside; remember death and decay, and cease from sin" (Sir 28:6 NABRE). The Christian has a two-fold reason for frequently pondering and even meditating upon death: first, because it helps him see the vanity of temporal goods which will one day be lost; and second, because death is the door through which we will one day pass in order to see Jesus, the ultimate desire of our hearts.

Perhaps many Christians are reluctant and even afraid to think about death because they do not live in hope. They fear death as something which will deprive them of happiness, and so the possibility of a happy death seems meaningless to them. It is for this very reason that we should all have a greater devotion to Saint Joseph, patron of a happy death. Nothing removes our fear better than having a friend who leads us through the valley of the shadow of death because he himself once walked that path. A friend who knows what frightens us and will not leave our side. And that friend is Saint Joseph. If we pray to him often with fervor, he will obtain for us the grace to no longer fear death and, even more importantly, the grace of joy at the moment of our death.

Chapter 10

Guardian and Provider for the Souls in Purgatory

Since Saint Joseph had a happy death, it is natural to ask the question: Where did Saint Joseph go after his death? Death involves the separation of body and soul, and so there are actually two questions that need to be answered: Where did Saint Joseph's soul go, and where did his body go? In this chapter, we will answer the question about Saint Joseph's soul, and in the next chapter, we will answer the question about his body.

A good first guess about the destination of Saint Joseph's soul might be: he went to heaven, since that is where all the righteous go to experience perpetual bliss. And it is certainly true that heaven was Saint Joseph's final destination. But as we shall see, it was not possible yet for Saint Joseph or anyone else to go to heaven before Jesus ascended into heaven. Jesus had to be the firstfruits of our race and the first to enter into heaven. Saint Paul addresses it here: "But now Christ has been raised from the dead, the firstfruits of those who have fallen asleep. For since death came through a man, the resurrection of the dead came also through a man. For just as in Adam all die, so too in Christ shall all be brought to life, but each one in proper order: Christ the firstfruits; then, at his coming, those who belong to Christ" (1 Cor 15:20–23 NABRE).

Many souls died in God's grace before Jesus's resurrection and ascension. But even though they were in God's grace, they could not enter into heaven and see the face of God until Christ led the way and opened the doors to heaven. The Church's liturgy clearly teaches this: "By his rising from the dead, he has opened the way to eternal life; and by ascending to you, O Father, he has unlocked the gates of heaven."[51] This opening of the door of heaven was signified by the rending of the veil at the death of Jesus: "Behold, the curtain of the temple was torn in two, from top to bottom" (Mt 27:51). This veil was embroidered with images of the cherubim[52] and so was an apt symbol of the door to heaven being opened. Saint Joseph was among those who died before the resurrection and ascension of Jesus, so he too had to wait somewhere else before entering into heaven.[53]

---

[51] Roman Missal, Preface IV for Sundays of Ordinary Time.

[52] See Ex 26:31; 36:35; 2 Chr 3:14.

[53] Someone might object to this assertion that no one entered into heaven before Christ's ascension. Two obvious difficulties are Elijah and the good thief. Elijah is said to have been brought into heaven when the flaming chariots took him (see 1 Mc 2:58). As for the good thief, Jesus said to him, "This day you shall be with me in paradise" (Lk 23:43). Saint Thomas Aquinas responds to these two cases separately. On the one hand, when it says that Elijah was taken up into heaven, this refers to the fact that the chariots brought him into the sky, but not into the eternal heaven of the blessed (according to Saint Thomas and some Fathers, he was eventually brought to the earthly paradise in the Garden of Eden to await the last days of the world). Regarding the good thief, Saint Thomas Aquinas says that since Jesus enlightened the just in the lower regions, paradise was temporarily in the lower regions during the days between our Lord's death and resurrection (*Summa Theologica*, IIIa, q.52, a.4, ad.3).

Saint Thomas Aquinas explains how and why the doors to heaven remained closed until Jesus ascended into heaven:

> Through the Passion of Christ, the human race is liberated not only from sin, but also from the debt of punishment. But men were bound to a debt of punishment in two ways: in one way on account of actual sin, which each one commits in his own person; in another way on account of the sin of the whole of human nature [original sin]. . . . The punishment due to original sin is bodily death and exclusion from the life of glory, as is clear from those things said in Genesis (ch. 2 and 3). . . . And, therefore, Christ, descending to the lower regions, by the power of his Passion, dissolved the debt by which they were excluded from the life of glory.[54]

Saint Thomas then cites the prophet Zechariah and Saint Paul's epistle to the Colossians to manifest that this is the teaching of Sacred Scripture: "For the blood of your covenant with me, I will bring forth your prisoners from the dungeon. In the return to the fortress of the waiting prisoners" (Zec 9:11–12 Vulgate); and "He brought you to life along with him, having forgiven us all our transgressions; obliterating the bond against us, with its legal claims, which was opposed to us, he also removed it from our midst, nailing it to the cross; despoiling the principalities and the powers, he made a public spectacle of them, leading them away in

[54] *Summa Theologiae*, IIIa, q.52, a.5.

triumph by it" (Col 2:13–15 NABRE). We can also add the text of Ephesians: "Grace was given to each of us according to the measure of Christ's gift. Therefore it is said, 'When he ascended on high he led a host of captives, and he gave gifts to men.' In saying, 'He ascended,' what does it mean but that he had also descended into the lower parts of the earth? He who descended is he who also ascended far above all the heavens, that he might fill all things" (Eph 4:7–10).

Who are the "prisoners" led forth from the dungeon? Who are the "host of captives" whom Christ led out upon His ascension? How were the principalities and powers despoiled? These texts indicate clearly that Jesus, after His death, led forth souls from a place of captivity in the "lower parts." This is what we confess each Sunday in the Creed when we affirm that He "descended into hell"[55] to release those in captivity.

So, immediately after His death, Jesus went to where the holy Fathers, including Saint Joseph, awaited His coming. Now at this point, it will be helpful to ask some questions and make some clarifications. Is the hell where Jesus descended the same hell where the damned now reside? Or was it purgatory, or limbo, or some other place or state? And was it a physical place? At the time of Jesus's death, there

[55] Apostle's Creed. The word "hell" is often misunderstood in this article of the Creed. People assume that hell only signifies the place of those who are eternally damned and undergoing sensible punishment. But in fact, the word hell has many senses in Scripture and Church teaching (some of which I will consider immediately below). The hell to which Jesus descended was not a place of torment for wicked people but a place of waiting for the just who had died before Jesus.

were four possible states of those who had died. I will briefly explain each state.[56]

First, there was the hell of the damned. Before Jesus's coming, if someone died unrepentant and in a state of mortal sin, they were condemned to the hell of the damned. In this hell, each soul suffers two punishments which are eternal. The first is eternal separation from God. The second is something like physical pain corresponding to their particular sins. Since these souls are eternally unrepentant, Jesus did not descend to save them. So Jesus did not descend into the hell of the damned, nor was Saint Joseph found there.

Second, there was limbo, which is the place where those who died only with original sin went. When a child, for example, died without grace, but also without any personal sin, this child was not incorporated into the mystical body of Christ (since grace is necessary for this). But because they did not commit any actual personal sins, they also do not deserve any physical punishment. So their condition is a state of natural joy akin to the condition of Adam and Eve in the Garden of Eden. Nevertheless, the beatific vision is not possible for these souls since the beatific vision is not a reward simply for not sinning but rather a reward for loving God with supernatural charity. And since these souls

---

[56] I shall refer to each of these four possibilities as "states." This is not to deny that there were physical places associated with each of these states. For example, the very fact that there are bodies in heaven show that heaven is not only a state but also a place. The same could be said about hell after the final judgment. But I use the term "state" in order to indicate that the primary truth about them is not where they are but rather the condition in which the souls found themselves in relation to God and their salvation.

were not destined for the life of glory, Jesus did not descend to limbo.[57]

The third possible state of a soul who had died before the ascension of Jesus was purgatory.[58] Before the coming of Christ, it was possible to receive grace by means of faith in Christ who was yet to come. For example, faithful Jews of the Old Testament who believed in what was prophesied about Christ in the Scriptures and who used the sign delivered to Abraham (circumcision) could live in the grace of Christ. Yet, if their love for Christ was not perfect at the time of their death, these souls still had need of purification on account of venial sins or forgiven mortal sins. And so they underwent some kind of punishment which served as a purgation or satisfaction while they awaited the coming of Jesus. When Jesus descended after His death, He came to these souls as Saint Peter expressly teaches: "For Christ also suffered for sins once, the righteous for the sake of the unrighteous, that he might lead you to God. Put to death in the flesh, he was brought to life in the spirit. In it he also went to preach to the spirits in prison, who had once been

---

[57] It is important to realize that it is possible for a child who is not baptized to be saved by some extraordinary intervention of Christ. Those infants who die without baptism, through no fault of theirs or their parents, are not bound to the ordinary sacramental order. However, the Church has no revelation about how Christ might save such children. So the Church simply entrusts these to the mercy of God who loves these children more than their own parents.

[58] In order not to detract from the overall flow of the argument, I will not defend the existence of purgatory as understood in Catholic teaching here. However, I have placed an explanation of the Catholic doctrine of purgatory together with an argument for the existence of purgatory in the appendix.

disobedient while God patiently waited in the days of Noah" (1 Pt 3:18–20 NABRE).

That is, Christ went down to those souls who had been disobedient but made an act of faith in Christ and an act of perfect contrition before they were drowned in the flood. So they were saved but still had some sins for which they had to atone. When Christ descended into hell, some of these souls, benefiting from the merits of His passion, were liberated from purgatory and brought with Christ to heaven at his ascension.

Finally, the fourth possible state was the hell of the Fathers (namely, those just and saintly men and women who had faith in Christ who was to come, and who loved Christ with a perfect love). This hell (much different from the typical notion of hell) was the place where those saints who died in God's grace and without need of purification went. Although these souls were morally perfect and did not suffer any punishment for their personal sins, nevertheless, they retained the guilt or debt of original sin, since Christ had not yet freed them from this debt. And part of this debt was exclusion from the life of glory and the vision of God. Therefore, Christ descended first for these souls to lead them into heaven at His ascension. After His ascension, this state no longer is possible since every soul who is perfect in charity at death since the ascension of Christ immediately enters into heaven.

From these considerations, we can see why Saint Joseph did not immediately enter heaven at his death. Instead, he entered into this fourth state, the hell of the Fathers. And there he awaited the coming of Jesus. But while he was there, what was he doing? Some insight into this question is found in the spiritual sense of a text about the life of Joseph the patriarch.

Typological Argument That Saint Joseph Was Placed Over the Souls Who Await Christ

When reading Joseph the patriarch's life, we find that he was cast into prison on account of the fault of someone else. The wife of Potiphar convinced her husband that Joseph was guilty of sin. So Potiphar had Joseph sent to prison. The text continues: "And Joseph's master took him and put him into the prison, the place where the king's prisoners were confined, and he was there in prison. But the Lord was with Joseph and showed him steadfast love, and gave him favor in the sight of the keeper of the prison. And the keeper of the prison committed to Joseph's care all the prisoners who were in the prison; and whatever was done there, he was the doer of it; the keeper of the prison paid no heed to anything that was in Joseph's care, because the Lord was with him; and whatever he did, the Lord made it prosper" (Gn 39:20–23).

Granted that Joseph is a type of Saint Joseph, how does this event in his life prefigure something about Saint Joseph's life? The first thing worth noting is that both Joseph the patriarch and Saint Joseph were once cast into prison. Joseph the patriarch was cast into a prison in Egypt while on earth. Saint Joseph was cast into a prison in the hell of the Fathers after death. Saint Peter described this prison when he said that Christ went "and preached to the spirits in prison" (1 Pt 3:19). Moreover, since Saint Joseph was not guilty of any personal sin, but only original sin, he was cast into that prison on account of the sin of a woman (Eve) and her husband who believed her (Adam). Once those parallels are clear, it becomes evident how to interpret the remainder of the text: the chief jailer is God, in whose hands are the souls of all the dead. And God places Saint Joseph over all of the souls in the prison, entrusting everything to his care. Clearly, Saint Joseph was placed over the souls who, in death, awaited the coming of Christ. Notice that the text says that Joseph was placed in the prison where all the "royal prisoners" were confined. Thus, these prisoners were the servants of the king (i.e., the souls in purgatory and the hell of the Fathers). Among these souls were Adam, Abraham, Isaac, Jacob, and all the holy ones of the Old Covenant.

Theological Arguments from the New Testament That Saint Joseph Is Guardian of the Souls in Purgatory

Turning to the New Testament, we now seek to discover if any further conclusions can be reached through a typological argument. At least two arguments from the New Testament confirm the conclusion that Saint Joseph was guardian over the souls in purgatory. The first argument can be summarized as follows: Saint Joseph was the holiest of the souls among the dead awaiting the coming of Christ. But in the next life, God confers the greatest authority over those who are holiest. Therefore, after his death, Saint Joseph was granted the greatest authority among the dead.

We established the truth of the first premise concerning Saint Joseph's holiness in chapter five. This conclusion has been confirmed by the magisterium of the Church: "There can be no doubt but that Joseph approached as no other person ever could that eminent dignity whereby the Mother of God towers above all creatures."[59] So the main premise we have to argue for is the second premise of this argument—namely, that in the next life God confers the greatest authority over those who are holiest.

The position that God grants the greatest authority to those who live the most virtuous lives is likely on the face of it. It would be strange, for example, for those who are farther from God to rule over those who are closer to Him. The fact that this often happens in this life is a cause for many problems in the Church and in the world. Nor can we simply say that no one rules anyone else in the next life, since Jesus often taught the opposite, as when He said to His apostles: "As my Father appointed a kingdom for me, so do I appoint for you that you may eat and drink at my table in my kingdom, and sit on thrones judging the twelve tribes of Israel" (Lk 22:29–30). So it corresponds to our sense of justice that the best people should have the most authority.

Jesus also indicates that those who are holier and humbler shall exercise the greater authority in the life to come. He says that "whoever obeys and teaches these commandments will be called greatest in the kingdom of heaven" (Mt 5:19 NABRE); and that "the one who is least among all of you is the one who is the greatest" (Lk 9:48 NABRE). When the disciples were arguing about who was the greatest, Jesus taught them that "if anyone would be first, he must be last of all and servant of all" (Mk 9:35).

This same truth can be inferred from the parable of the talents (see Lk 19:12–19). In this parable, the one who made

---

[59] Pope Saint John Paul II, *Redemptoris Custos* no. 20.

more from his one talent received more authority. So also, the one who does greater good in this life with the same gifts from God seems to be holier. So we see from this parable also that the holier the person, the greater the authority he will exercise in the life to come. Now, if Saint Joseph was the holiest of the saints after Our Lady, and in the next life he was holiest among the souls of the dead waiting for Christ, it makes sense that Saint Joseph was preeminent in authority over those souls.

Now, someone might respond to this claim with the objection: "Yes, it is true that in heaven some exercise greater authority than others, but there is no evidence that this was so among the dead who had yet to enter heaven. So while he was among the dead in the hell of the Fathers, Saint Joseph exercised no special authority." This objection fails to keep in mind that the dead in Christ are also among the members of the Church. For there is the Church militant on earth, the Church triumphant in heaven, and the Church suffering in the abode of the dead. And wherever you find the Church, you find order and authority, since the order of charity endures beyond this life into the next, whether in heaven or in purgatory, since "love is strong as death" (Sg 8:6). Moreover, Scripture is clear that even among the dead who are not yet in heaven, some exercise authority over others. Consider this passage from Luke 16: "The poor man died and was carried by the angels to Abraham's bosom. The rich man also died and was buried; and in Hades, being in torment, he lifted up his eyes, and saw Abraham far off and Lazarus in his bosom. And he called out, 'Father Abraham, have mercy upon me, and send Lazarus to dip the end of his finger in water and cool my tongue; for I am in anguish in this flame'" (Lk 16:22–24).

In this passage, Jesus is speaking about the abode of the dead before His own resurrection. So they are not in heaven. Hence, Lazarus is not said to be carried to heaven but to the bosom of Abraham. Yet, in this abode of the dead, Abraham not only has authority over the rich man but also over Lazarus. For why would the rich man ask for a benefit from Abraham and call him father unless he acknowledged that Abraham had some authority over him? And why would Lazarus be sent by Abraham unless Abraham had the authority to send him?

So our original conclusion still stands: the holier the person, the more authority he exercises in the life to come (even among the dead). But Saint Joseph was the holiest among the dead. Therefore, Saint Joseph exercised the greatest authority among those who had died. And since he has entered into heaven, Saint Joseph's authority has not diminished but only increased. Therefore, he remains a special protector and guardian over the souls who are today in purgatory. This sheds light upon the doctrine that Saint Joseph is the patron of the universal Church. For his patronage extends not only over those on earth in the Church militant but also over those in purgatory in the Church suffering.

Another Argument from Scripture

Besides the argument from Joseph's holiness, we can reach the same conclusion from Christ's very words. Specifically, these words are contained in the following passage about the finding of Jesus in the temple:

> Now his parents went to Jerusalem every year at the feast of the Passover. And when he was twelve years old, they went up according to custom; and when the feast was ended, as they were returning, the boy Jesus stayed behind in Jerusalem. His parents did not know it, but supposing him to be in the company they went a day's journey, and they sought him among their kinsfolk and acquaintances; and when they did not find him, they returned to Jerusalem, seeking him. After three days they found him in the temple, sitting among the teachers, listening to them and asking them questions; and all who heard him were amazed at his understanding and his answers. And when they saw him they were astonished; and his mother said to the child, "Son, why did you act to us in this way? Behold, your father and I have been seeking you sorrowfully." And he said to them, "Why is it that you were seeking me? Did you not know that it is necessary that I be in my Father's house?" And they did not understand the saying which he spoke to them. And he went down with them and came to Nazareth, and was obedient to them; and his mother kept all the sayings in her heart. (Lk 2:41–51 Vulgate)

At first glance, this passage seems to indicate nothing regarding Saint Joseph's relationship to the souls in purgatory. But as so often happens with Sacred Scripture, a careful reading of the text reveals much more than what appears on the surface. When Mary asks Jesus "Son, why did you act to us in this way?" Jesus replies, as He so often does, with another question: "Why is it that you were seeking me? Did you not know that it is necessary that I be in my Father's house?" But "they did not understand the saying which he spoke to them." What exactly did Mary and Joseph not understand? A superficial reading of the text might lead someone to think that they did not understand that God was His Father. But that is an impossible reading. How could Mary not know that God was Jesus's Father when this was revealed directly to her by the angel? The same holds true of Joseph.

To understand more clearly what was mysterious about Jesus's words to them, we must pay careful attention to the precise words of this text. Saint Luke records two unusual expressions which carry a deeper meaning. First, when explaining to his parents why He had acted in this way towards them, Jesus uses the expression *it was necessary* (δει) that He be in His Father's house. It is obvious that Jesus was perfectly free to go with His parents rather than stay back in Jerusalem in the Temple. So how can Jesus say this act freely chosen by Him was necessary?

The second unusual expression which Saint Luke records is that Mary and Joseph did not understand *the saying* (το ρημα), then adds that His mother kept all *the sayings* (τα ρηματα) in her heart. While this seems to be a common expression, in fact, when used with the definite article *the* (το), it has quite a precise meaning in Saint Luke's Gospel, as well as in other places in Scripture.

Let us first examine the significance of Jesus's assertion that *it was necessary* that He be in His Father's house. This is not a unique instance of Jesus speaking about a free or possible future action as necessary. In fact, Jesus speaks this way many times throughout the Gospels;[60] and in Saint Luke's Gospel at least nine times does Jesus speak as if free or possible future actions are necessary.[61] In most of these cases, Jesus is speaking about the necessity surrounding the events of His passion, death, and resurrection (though in a few instances he is speaking about the end of the world). But in each case, Jesus uses this language of necessity to indicate the relationship between a prophecy or prophetic act and its fulfillment. In other words, this language of necessity expresses the order of divine providence: an order which is known to Jesus. It will be helpful to see some examples. When Jesus is about to be arrested, Saint Matthew records this event in the Garden of Gethsemane: "And behold, one of those who were with Jesus stretched out his hand and drew his sword, and struck the slave of the high priest, and cut off his ear. Then Jesus said to him, 'Put your sword back into its place; for all who take the sword will perish by the sword. Do you think that I cannot appeal to my Father, and he will at once send me more than twelve legions of angels? But how then should the scriptures be fulfilled, that it is necessary (δει) to be so?'" (Mt 26:51–54 Vulgate).

Jesus asserts here that He could have called upon His Father to rescue Him. But if He had done so, this would have prevented the Scriptures from being fulfilled. And in Jesus's mind, it is necessary that the Scriptures be fulfilled since they express the fullness of the divine plan.

60 See Mt 16:21; Mt 26:54; Mk 8:31; Jn 12:34; Jn 20:9.

61 See Lk 9:22; 13:33; 17:25; 22:7, 22:37; 24:7, 26, 44.

Again, in Saint Luke's account of the Passion we find this text: "[Jesus] said to them, 'But now, let him who has a purse take it, and likewise a bag. And let him who has no sword sell his mantle and buy one. For I tell you that it is necessary (δει) that this scripture be fulfilled in me: "And he was reckoned with transgressors." For what is written about me has its fulfilment'" (Lk 22:36–37 Vulgate).

Here, again, Jesus speaks about the necessary relationship between scriptural prophecy and its fulfillment. When Jesus says that it was necessary that He be in his Father's house, He is asserting that there is something prophetic about Him being in His Father's house.

The use of the expression *the saying* (using the definite article) confirms this prophetic understanding of Jesus's action. Saint Luke had already used this expression twice before in his Gospel. When the angel Gabriel first spoke to Mary with the words "Hail full of grace, the Lord is with you," she was "greatly troubled at *the saying*" (Lk 1:28–29). Later on, the shepherds "made known *the saying* which had been told them concerning this child" (Lk 2:17). In both cases, the expression *the saying* refers to a prophetic word which is later understood by those to whom it was spoken. Similar instances are found in the other Gospels as well. Saint Mark records that Jesus said to His apostles, "'The Son of man will be delivered into the hands of men, and they will kill him; and when he is killed, after three days he will rise.' But they did not understand *the saying*, and they were afraid to ask him" (Mk 9:31–32). Similarly, Saint Matthew records that "Peter remembered *the saying* of Jesus, 'Before the cock crows, you will deny me three times.' And he went out and wept bitterly" (Mt 26:75). In these instances, the expression *the saying* refers specifically to a prophetic word which will become more fully understood later by those to whom it is spoken.

So when Jesus says to Mary and Joseph that it was necessary that He be in His Father's house, Jesus is clearly speaking a prophetic word to them and referring to His choice to be in His Father's house as a prophetic act. Moreover, the implication is that they will understand its meaning in the future. Perhaps this is why Saint Luke adds that Mary "kept all the sayings in her heart" as if to imply that she was storing them up in order to understand their meaning later.

Since this is the case, can we discover the meaning of this prophetic act and identify its fulfillment later in Scripture? In the Old Testament, many of the prophets performed prophetic acts: acts which signified some future reality.[62] The prophetic significance of these acts depended upon the likenesses which existed between the prophetic act and its fulfillment. An example from the life of the prophet Ezekiel will serve to illustrate:

> The word of the Lord came to me: "Son of man, you dwell in the midst of a rebellious house, who have eyes to see, but see not, who have ears to hear, but hear not; for they are a rebellious house. Therefore, son of man, prepare for yourself an exile's baggage, and go into exile by day in their sight; you shall go like an

[62] To cite some well-known examples, Ezekiel does not mourn his wife as a prophetic act (Ez 24:16–26). Jeremiah buries his loincloth as a prophetic act (Jer 13:1–11) and breaks a clay vessel into shards as a prophetic act (Jer 19:10).

> exile from your place to another place in their sight. Perhaps they will understand, though they are a rebellious house. You shall bring out your baggage by day in their sight, as baggage for exile; and you shall go forth yourself at evening in their sight, as men do who must go into exile. Dig through the wall in their sight, and go out through it. In their sight you shall lift the baggage upon your shoulder, and carry it out in the dark; you shall cover your face, that you may not see the land; for I have made you a sign for the house of Israel." And I did as I was commanded. I brought out my baggage by day, as baggage for exile, and in the evening I dug through the wall with my own hands; I went forth in the dark, carrying my outfit upon my shoulder in their sight. In the morning, the word of the Lord came to me: "Son of man, has not the house of Israel, the rebellious house, said to you, 'What are you doing?' Say to them: 'Thus says the LORD GOD: This oracle concerns the prince in Jerusalem and all the house of Israel who are in it.' Say: 'I am a sign for you: as I have done, so shall it be done to them; they shall go into exile, into captivity.' And the prince who is among them shall lift his baggage upon his shoulder in the dark, and shall go forth; he shall dig through the wall and go out through it; he shall cover his face, that he may not see the land with his eyes." (Ez 12:1–12)

In this instance, Ezekiel performed a similar act to what the Israelites would do in the future. Just as he lifted his baggage in the dark, so would they. Just as he dug a hole in the wall, so would they. Just as he covered his face so he could not see the land as he fled, so would they. The act was so much like its fulfillment that it was clearly a prophecy of what was to come.

Applying this principle to the prophetic act of the losing and finding of Jesus in the temple, we are now in a better position to discover how the pascal mystery: Jesus's death, descent to the dead, and resurrection was the fulfillment of this prophetic act. Consider these likenesses:

1. The pascal mystery began at the time of the Passover in Jerusalem. Jesus and His parents were in Jerusalem for the Passover.
2. Jesus was lost to His sorrowing mother for three days. Jesus was lost to His sorrowing parents for three days.
3. During those three days, Jesus was preaching to and instructing the souls of the dead (see 1 Pt 3:19). Jesus was teaching the elders in his Father's house during those three days.
4. After His resurrection, those who were seeking Him were asked why they were seeking the living among the dead (Lk 24:5). After He is found, Mary and Joseph were asked by Jesus why they were seeking Him.

These distinct likenesses, together with the prophetic language recorded by Saint Luke, provide evidence that the finding of Jesus in the temple was mysteriously pointing ahead to Jesus's pascal mystery. They also help explain why two persons as spiritually advanced as Mary and Joseph could not initially understand the meaning of Jesus's words.

We are now in a position to return to the original question of this section: Does the finding of Jesus in the temple clearly reveal anything about Saint Joseph's status in relation to the souls of those who have died but are not yet in heaven? A careful examination of the third likeness above shows that the three days Jesus spent in the temple teaching corresponds to the three days Jesus spent among the dead teaching. But notice that Jesus does not call the place where He is teaching "the temple." Instead, He calls it His "Father's house." This implies that the abode of the dead was also His father's house—namely, the house of Joseph, since Joseph was preeminent among the dead. Just as the abode of the dead had once been called Abraham's bosom to indicate Abraham's paternal care over the souls of the dead, Jesus now indicates by a prophetic word that when He descends among the dead it will instead be called his father's house, since Joseph will have supplanted Abraham as the father who will care for the souls of all the dead.

Devotion to Saint Joseph, Guardian of the Souls in Purgatory

Saint Joseph's role as a special guardian over the souls in purgatory is confirmed in the practice of the faith and the belief of many saints. Blessed Mary of Providence founded a religious order dedicated to assist the souls in purgatory, the Helpers of the Souls in Purgatory, and she placed it under Saint Joseph's patronage. She promised that if he would assist her in this undertaking, the first statue erected at the new house would be in honor of him. The day after a residence had been acquired, a benefactor, who had known nothing of the promise, promptly delivered a statue of Saint Joseph. Saint Joseph once said to Servant of God Sister Mary Martha Chambon, "If the soul who prayed to me still has debts to pay to the Sovereign Judge, I shall ask for grace on its behalf."[63]

All Catholics have a solemn duty to assist the souls in purgatory. And this duty is more urgent for those of us who likely have loved ones among those holy souls. They cannot help themselves, but we can help them by our prayers and sacrifices: especially indulgenced prayers and Masses. The theological conclusions of this chapter also show that entrusting our loved ones to Saint Joseph and imploring his intercession for the souls in purgatory will greatly amplify the effects of our own prayers. Moreover, those of us who have had a special devotion to Saint Joseph in this life can hope to expect a superabundance of help from him in the life to come. In this life, and in the life to come, God has provided Saint Joseph to us as a loving father.

---

[63] *Mystic of the Holy Wounds: The Life and Revelations of Sr. Mary Martha Chambon*, trans. Ryan P. Plummer (St. Louis, MO: Lambfount, 2019), 98.

Chapter 11

Saint Joseph Assumed into Heaven, Body and Soul

Now that we have considered the destiny and state of Saint Joseph's soul after his happy death, we turn to a consideration of the destiny and state of his body after his death. Is it possible that Saint Joseph, like Mary, was assumed body and soul into heaven? While faith in the bodily assumption of the Blessed Virgin Mary was practically ubiquitous in the early Church, the same cannot be said about belief that Saint Joseph was assumed bodily into heaven. There may be some very practical reasons for this uncertainty. Saint Joseph would have died before Jesus began His public ministry, so he was not well-known to the first community of Christians, nor is it likely that his burial place was well-known or venerated by the early community of Christians. In contrast, Mary, the Mother of the Lord, was in constant contact with the early Christian community, and her death would have been known to virtually all Christians at the time. So the astounding events surrounding her death would also have become public so that faith in her bodily assumption would have immediately taken root in the newborn Church.

Nevertheless, as the centuries passed and the faithful began to show greater interest in the person of Saint Joseph, certain telling facts began to emerge. For example, there were no reliable accounts about his relics, and no church seriously claims to possess his body: something strange given the penchant for the early Christians to venerate relics of everything sacred related to the life of the Lord Jesus.

Moreover, as a deeper understanding of Saint Joseph's holiness began to take shape in the Church's theology, it became reasonable to ask if there were certain privileges granted to Saint Joseph as a sign of his eminent holiness. As a result, many saints, whether through theological reasoning or through private revelations, began to assert Saint Joseph's bodily assumption into heaven was among the prerogatives given to him. Among these saints we can list Bernadine of Siena, Vincent Ferrer, Francis de Sales, and Pope John XXIII. For example, Pope Saint John XXIII wrote: "We may piously believe—Jesus allowed [Saint Joseph] the honor and the privilege to admirably accompany him on the path to heaven (on the day of his Ascension) and to sing the first notes of the never ending hymn, 'Te Deum.'"[64]

Saint Francis De Sales, a Doctor of the Church, taught this doctrine persuasively:

> Storks provide a true picture of the mutual piety of children for their parents and parents for their children. They are birds of passage and they carry their aged fathers and mothers on their journeys, just as when they were small their own fathers and mothers

[64] Homily on the Ascension given on May 26, 1960.

> had carried them on like occasions. Who can doubt that when this holy father came to the end of his years, he, in turn, was carried by his divine foster Child on his journey from this world into the next, into Abraham's bosom, from there to be translated into the Son's own bosom, into glory, on the day of his Ascension?[65]

Given that there is a germ of faith in this teaching budding in the Church today, it is worthwhile to search the Sacred Scriptures for evidence of this fact.

Typological Argument That Saint Joseph Was Assumed Bodily into Heaven

When we look to the primary type of Saint Joseph in the Old Testament, Joseph the patriarch, we find a reference which clearly can be understood as a type of Saint Joseph's preservation from corruption and bodily assumption into heaven. Consider the following texts from Genesis and Exodus:

> And Joseph said to his brothers, "I am about to die; but God will visit you, and bring you up out of this land to the land which he swore to Abraham, to Isaac, and to Jacob." Then Joseph took an oath of the sons of Israel, saying, "God will visit you, and you shall carry up my bones from here." So Joseph died, being a hundred and ten years old; and they embalmed him, and he was put in a coffin in Egypt. (Gn 50:24–26)

---

[65] *Treatise on Divine Love*, Bk. 7, ch.13. See also his statement on the same topic in *Les Vrais Entretiens Spirituels*.

> And Moses took the bones of Joseph with him; for Joseph had solemnly sworn the people of Israel, saying, "God will visit you; then you must carry my bones with you from here." (Ex 13:19)

Notable too is the brief passage from Sirach about Joseph, which sums up a life which took thirteen entire chapters of Genesis to record with the brief encomium: "Was ever a man born like Joseph? Even his dead body was provided for" (Sir 49:15 NABRE).[66] The provision for his dead body seems to refer both to its embalming and to its translation into the Promised Land.

The first noticeable feature about these texts is that Joseph was embalmed. Embalming was a common practice for Egyptian royalty, and it caused a kind of incorruptibility of the body. Joseph's bodily incorruption after death has obvious typological implications for Saint Joseph's body after his death—namely, that God preserved his body from corruption, in imitation of Christ, about whom it was prophesied: "You shall not permit your faithful one to undergo corruption" (Ps 16:10 Vulgate). This already implies a kind of proximate preparation for heavenly glory.

But not only is Joseph embalmed, his body is carried into the Promised Land at the time when God visits His people. It is well known that the Promised Land is a type of heaven. It is described as a land flowing with milk and honey, and a

---

[66] Interestingly, the Vulgate text for this passage is quite different. It reads: "Joseph was a man born prince of his brethren, the support of his family, the ruler of his brethren, the stay of the people. And his bones were visited, and after death they prophesied."

perpetual inheritance of God's people. Its capital is Jerusalem, the city of peace, which is a type of the New Jerusalem, the city described in the book of Revelation as the dwelling of God's elect in heaven. So it is easy to see how the bearing of the body of Joseph into the Promised Land is a type of Saint Joseph's assumption into heaven. In fact, the text most often used to refer to Our Lady's bodily assumption into heaven uses a similar figure: "Arise O Lord, into your resting place: you and the ark, which you have sanctified" (Ps 131:8 Vulgate). In context, this passage refers to the bringing of the ark into Jerusalem. Just as in the text about the body of Joseph being carried into the Promised Land, in this text also the ark, a type of Mary, was carried into Jerusalem, a type of heaven, to signify her bodily assumption.

We should also note the significance of the timing of the carrying of the body of Joseph into the Promised Land. Joseph says that this will take place when God visits His people. This phrase signifies a time of mercy and salvation. And the two times which most clearly reflect God's visitation are Jesus's resurrection and His return in glory at the end of the world. Therefore, implied in this text is the reality that Saint Joseph would be assumed into heaven at the time of Jesus's resurrection.

Elijah the Prophet

Perhaps the most convincing typological evidence for Saint Joseph's bodily assumption is found in the prophet Elijah. At the end of his earthly journey, Elijah was carried up to the sky in a fiery chariot. The second book of Kings records this event succinctly. Elisha, the disciple of Elijah, accompanied his master all the way to the far side of the Jordan (not far from the place where Jesus was baptized). There, "as they still went on and talked, behold, a chariot of fire and horses of fire separated the two of them. And Elijah went up by a whirlwind into heaven. And Eli′sha saw it and he cried, 'My father, my father! the chariots of Israel and its horsemen'" (2 Kgs 2:11–12). The book of Sirach reports the same event in these words: "You who were taken up by a whirlwind of fire, in a chariot with horses of fire; you who are ready at the appointed time, it is written, to calm the wrath of God before it breaks out in fury, to turn the heart of the father to the son" (Sir 48:9–10).

Many fathers of the Church interpret this second text in conjunction with the two witnesses mentioned in Revelation 11 as indicating that Elijah will reappear at the end of the world. But also worthy of mentioning is Elijah's connection with fatherhood. Elijah was a spiritual father, and so he is specially endowed with the power to turn the hearts of fathers towards their children. About whom could this more truly be said than about Saint Joseph?

In any case, Elijah's assumption into the heavens is a clear type of the bodily assumption of Saint Joseph. Indeed, it would be difficult to find a type which could be clearer!

Theological Arguments for Saint Joseph's Bodily Assumption Based upon New Testament Texts

At this point, I want to be a little careful in asserting too much about what the New Testament texts clearly reveal about Saint Joseph's bodily assumption. There's an old Latin saying: *Qui probat nimis probat nihil*, which translates as: He who proves too much proves nothing. It seems to me that the arguments in this section for Saint Joseph's bodily assumption are more arguments from fittingness and are partial, rather than complete, demonstrations. Nevertheless, this is already to advance the theological conversation on this matter. I am convinced upon the strength of the typological evidence for Saint Joseph's bodily assumption that a strict demonstration can ultimately be constructed from the New Testament texts.

The first New Testament text we should consider is the mysterious text of Matthew 27 recording the death of Jesus: "The earth shook, and the rocks were split; the tombs also were opened, and many bodies of the saints who had fallen asleep were raised, and coming out of the tombs after his resurrection they went into the holy city and appeared to many" (Mt 27:51–53).

Now this text speaks specifically of many saints. And it does not specify that this resurrection was a resurrection to glory. Perhaps it was merely a resurrection to this life again, as happened when Jesus raised Lazarus from the dead. Still, there is also good reason to suppose that this text may be referring to a resurrection to glory. For the text says that after their resurrection, they "appeared to many." Now if they were only resurrected back to this state of life like Lazarus, the use of the word "appeared" seems strange. One expects the text to say that they were reunited with their loved ones or returned to their families, or something of that sort. But instead, it refers to their resurrection in a way similar to the references to Jesus's resurrection.[67] Moreover, it says that they entered "the holy city." This name for Jerusalem calls to mind its prefigurement of the heavenly Jerusalem spoken about in Revelation 21–22 and Isaiah 52. These texts suggest that Saint Matthew is likely writing about a resurrection to glory. And it is quite possible that more than one saint was granted this privilege. Who is more likely to be among these resurrected ones than Saint Joseph?

But the most significant New Testament text which seems to point clearly to Saint Joseph's bodily resurrection is when Mary and Joseph find Jesus in the temple. In the previous chapter, we established this passage is prophetic, and that it bears several striking likenesses to the Paschal Mystery of Christ, including His resurrection. Recall that the passage includes elements prefiguring the Passion of the Lord after Passover in Jerusalem; elements prefiguring the death and descent of the Lord to the dead where, for three days, He went to instruct in His father's house; and elements prefiguring His resurrection, including the same question asked of those seeking the Christ: "Why were you seeking?" Does this passage not point to the reality that when Jesus rose from the dead, a reunion of the Holy Family occurred, just as there had been a reunion at His finding in the temple which prefigured His resurrection? If this is so, as I believe it is, then we can conclude that after Jesus had been among the dead in this father's house (the hell of the Fathers), He brought His father Joseph with Him, resurrected and glorified, to be reunited with His mother Mary before they both ascended into heaven.

---

[67] Cf. Lk 24:34; Mk 16:9–14 where Jesus is also said to appear to his disciples.

This interpretation also helps to explain the significance of the statement that Mary "kept all these sayings in her heart." For in the other cases in the Gospels where someone is said to recall or keep a prophetic saying, that same person witnesses its fulfillment in a way to understand what had been prophesied earlier. For example, "Peter remembered *the saying* of Jesus: 'before the cock crows, you will deny me three times.' And he went out and wept bitterly" (Mt 26:75). That is, Peter saw and understood the fulfillment of Jesus's prophetic word. The episode of the shepherds is even clearer:

> When the angels went away from them into heaven, the shepherds said to one another: "Let us go over to Bethlehem and see this thing that has happened, which the Lord has made known to us." And they went with haste, and found Mary and Joseph, and the babe lying in a manger. And when they saw it they made known *the saying* which had been told them concerning this child; and all who heard it wondered at what the shepherds told them. But Mary kept all *the sayings*, pondering them in her heart. And the shepherds returned, glorifying and praising God for all they had *heard and seen, as it had been said to them.* (Lk 2:15–20)

The shepherds not only heard the saying but also saw its fulfillment. So it is very likely that even though it was not recorded directly in Scripture, Mary too saw the fulfillment of the prophetic act and saying of Jesus. The event of her reunion with Jesus and Joseph after His resurrection would have obviously been a very intimate and private moment for Mary. So rather than directly record its fulfillment, Saint Luke simply alludes to it in its prophetic form and adds that Mary kept it in her heart, implying that she somehow witnessed its fulfillment.

Additional Arguments for Saint Joseph's Bodily Assumption

In addition to the texts we have just considered, we can also make other arguments based upon various saints' writings and New Testament texts. One argument proceeds from the way in which Saint Joseph cooperated actively to preserve the virginity of his spouse, Mary. When we look at the early patristic arguments for Mary's bodily assumption into heaven, we notice that they are based not only upon her freedom from original sin but also upon her virginal integrity. The Byzantine liturgy prays, "As he kept you a virgin in childbirth, thus has he kept your body incorrupt in the tomb and has glorified it by his divine act of transferring it from the tomb."[68] Saint John Damascene wrote, "It was fitting that she who had kept her virginity intact in childbirth, should keep her own body free from all corruption even after death. It was fitting that she who had carried the Creator as a child at her breast, should dwell in the divine tabernacles."[69] And Saint Germanus of Constantinople wrote, "Your virginal body is all holy, all chaste, entirely the dwelling place of God, so that it is henceforth completely exempt from dissolution into dust. Though still human, it is changed into a heavenly life of incorruptibility, truly living and glorious, undamaged and sharing in perfect life."[70]

---

[68] *Menaei Totius Anni.*

[69] *Encomium in Dormitionem Dei Genetricis Semperque Virginis Mariae,* Hom. II, n.14.

[70] In *Sanctae Dei Genetricis Dormitionem,* Sermon I.

These texts indicate that Mary's virginal integrity was a reason for the incorruptibility and exaltation of her body. Saint Joseph actively contributed to this integrity by choosing not to exercise his marital rights over her virginal body. So it is fitting that Saint Joseph receive a reward proportionate to his contribution. Not only is Saint Joseph virginal, but he also participates in her virginal integrity and merits. Therefore, it is probable that by Mary's prayers, and as a reward for contributing to her virginal integrity, Saint Joseph remained incorrupt and was assumed bodily into heaven.

A further argument can be made from Christ's filial piety towards His father. Pope Pius XII argued that Mary's bodily assumption was the effect of Jesus's filial piety: "Out of filial love for his mother, Jesus Christ willed that she be assumed into heaven."[71] The same argument can be made for Saint Joseph, since Jesus also bore filial piety towards him and honored him in keeping with the fourth commandment.

Moreover, the reward for a virtuous act should somehow correspond to the good done. But Joseph preserved the body of the child Jesus from harm at the hands of Herod. Therefore, it is fitting that Jesus preserved the body of His father Joseph from corruption and decay at the hands of the devil.

Finally, it is appropriate that the origin of the heavenly life should mirror the origin of the first creation, since grace builds upon and perfects nature. Saint Paul implies this when he writes: "The first man was from the earth, earthly; the second man, from heaven. As was the earthly one, so also are the earthly, and as is the heavenly one, so also are the heavenly. Just

[71] *Munificentissimus Deus*, no. 25.

as we have borne the image of the earthly one, we shall also bear the image of the heavenly one" (1 Cor 15:47–49 NABRE).

At the beginning of our race there was a married couple, Adam and Eve. And when they had their first child, this couple became the original family. Therefore, it is most fitting that already in heaven there be, not only an individual, but a complete family (Joseph, Mary, and Jesus) who enjoys the firstfruits of eternal life. For Jesus was incarnate in a family, and so the fulfillment of His mission should be reflected in a family. As it was in the beginning, so shall it be in the end.

Devotion to Saint Joseph, Assumed into Heaven

The belief that Saint Joseph is now in heaven, body and soul, has important consequences for our moral lives. First, it reveals that our bodies are sacred temples of God's Spirit, sharing the same destiny as our souls. So often in the modern Church, many people act as if their souls and bodies are different realities, as if what we do with our bodies has little or no effect upon our souls.

Second, this belief teaches us that Mary, who was immaculately conceived, and thus free from original sin, is not the only one who enjoys the full beatitude of heaven in all the essential parts of her person and human nature. Joseph, too, even though he was for a time subject to original sin, has been rewarded with perfect blessedness even before the final judgment. Hence, we should already begin to live on earth the fullness of the heavenly life as much as possible. Not everyone had to wait until the end of the world to begin the fullness of the heavenly life.

Third, the fact that Saint Joseph is a complete person, body and soul, in heaven, makes him more tangible and approachable to the faithful. When we pray to a saint who is still awaiting their final resurrection, there can be a sense of distance not only because they have entered the next life but also because they are unlike us since their souls and bodies remain separated. But Mary and Joseph are like us: fully intact human persons, having body and soul.

Finally, the truth that the Holy Family, Jesus, Mary, and Joseph, are together enjoying the ultimate fruits of the heavenly life, already resurrected and interacting with one another with their human bodies and senses, reminds us that the destiny of the individual is largely bound up with the destiny of their family. In the Scriptures, Jesus raises the dead three times. And in each case, it was in response to the desires of an immediate family member: the daughter of Jairus, the son of the widow of Nain, and the brother of Martha and Mary. All the relationships within a human family are represented there: father/daughter, mother/son, brother/sister. Just as God gives natural life through the family, so also He normally bestows supernatural life through family members. This gives hope to those who are praying for the salvation of their family members. Remember, Saint Joseph was the weakest link and least holy member of the Holy Family, but through the prayers of his wife and child, he was brought into perfect heavenly glory with them.

Chapter 12

Consecration to Saint Joseph

In this last chapter, I will consider whether there is any scriptural evidence recommending consecration to Saint Joseph. But before examining the scriptural evidence for this, it is necessary to explain the nature and purpose of consecration to Jesus through a saint.

To consecrate someone or something is to make that person or thing holy. And holiness consists in union or conformity with Christ. Therefore, consecration is that which brings someone into closer conformity to Christ. Earlier, we met the objection that placing someone between us and Christ seems to put us at a greater distance from Christ. But as with a telescope, which is interposed between the eye and the heavens precisely to draw us closer to the heavens, so also with the mediation of the saints. Therefore, consecration to Saint Joseph means uniting and conforming ourselves to Joseph in order to be more closely united and perfectly conformed to Jesus.

Saint Louis Marie de Montfort once wrote the classic work on consecration, which taught the doctrine of consecration to Jesus through Mary: "Mary, being the most conformed of all creatures to Jesus Christ, it follows that, of all devotions, that which most consecrates and conforms our soul to Our Lord is devotion to his holy Mother; and that the more it is consecrated to Mary, the more it is consecrated to Jesus."[72]

Can the same be said about Saint Joseph? The answer is yes: we can become more conformed to Jesus by becoming more conformed to Joseph. For Joseph was the man who was closest to Christ, the man who pressed Jesus's tiny Sacred Heart against his own at Bethlehem, and rested his chaste heart on Jesus's breast while dying at Nazareth. Yes, Saint Joseph was the man who once held the Infant God and who himself was held by the God-man. We shall examine the scriptural evidence for Joseph conforming us to Jesus below. But if Saint Joseph leads us to Jesus, then consecration to Saint Joseph is a privileged means of drawing closer to Jesus.

In this context, we note that consecration to Joseph presupposes and builds upon consecration to Mary. Consecration to Joseph does not bypass consecration to Mary but builds upon it. The reason is quite simple: Joseph was related to Jesus through Mary. He could truly be called the father of Jesus only because he was the husband of Mary. So conformity to Saint Joseph will only bring us to conformity with Jesus through Mary.

Through marriage, Joseph mysteriously became the first person to consecrate himself to Mary, and his consecration was more profound and perfect than any since that time. We can easily deduce this truth from Saint Louis de Montfort's words on Marian consecration: "This devotion [consecration] consists, then, in giving ourselves entirely to Our Lady,

[72] *True Devotion to Mary*, Part II, ch.1, n.120.

in order to belong to Jesus through her. We must give her (1) our body, with all its senses and members; (2) our soul with all its powers; (3) our exterior goods of fortune whether present or to come; and (4) our interior and spiritual goods . . . in short, we must give her all we have."[73]

Who can be said to have given themselves more completely to Mary than Saint Joseph did when he married her? Marriage involves a total gift of self, and the consecration described by Saint Louis is clearly most perfectly found in a marriage.[74] And so, we find that consecration to Jesus through Joseph implies consecration to Jesus through Joseph *and* Mary.

There is one last theological question this raises: Can we consecrate ourselves to any saint? This is a fair question—perhaps requiring an answer that goes beyond this book's scope. But this much seems clear: because of the universal role Saint Joseph played and still plays in God's salvific plan, consecration to Saint Joseph can benefit every Catholic. Recall that Saint Joseph is the patron of the universal Church. This means that he has universal authority and jurisdiction over the whole order of grace, as the Genesis text implies: "without your consent no man shall lift up hand or foot in all the land of Egypt" (Gn 41:44). Thus it seems certain that consecration can be made to Saint Joseph, the saint who has some universal influence over all the elect.

---

[73] *True Devotion to Mary*, Part II, article one.

[74] Some saints have entered into a kind of mystical marriage with Our Lady in imitation of this profound consecration made by Saint Joseph. For example, the Norbertine Saint Herman Joseph was reported to have entered into such a consecration.

Typological Evidence for Consecration to Saint Joseph

Typological evidence for consecration to Saint Joseph can be found in the book of Genesis where it speaks about Joseph the patriarch. Joseph has entered Egypt and is now a servant to Potiphar, an Egyptian ruler. Here is the text: "So Joseph found favor in [Potiphar's] sight and attended him, and he made him overseer of his house and put him in charge of all that he had. From the time that he made him overseer in his house and over all that he had the Lord blessed the Egyptian's house for Joseph's sake; the blessing of the Lord was upon all that he had, in house and field. So he left all that he had in Joseph's charge" (Gn 39:4–6).

If we take Joseph as a type of Saint Joseph, the sense of the text is clear: the one who places Saint Joseph in charge of all that he has will be more abundantly blessed by the Lord in "house and field"—that is, in interior and exterior goods (such as an increase of wisdom and charity, and an increase of more effective good works). But to make Saint Joseph the overseer of our house, and to place Saint Joseph in charge of all we have, seems to signify nothing other than consecrating ourselves to Saint Joseph.

According to this interpretation, Potiphar can be understood to be a type of every Christian. But this poses a certain problem: Potiphar is Joseph's master. But we are not in authority over Saint Joseph. Therefore, this biblical interpretation seems unclear. In response, we can say that in this text, it is Joseph who is said to be the overseer and the one in charge, yet also that Joseph attended him. The same can be said about Saint Joseph in relation to us: before we give Saint Joseph this express authority over our goods, in some way we are still in charge of them. We are still master over our bodies and souls and their various goods. But once we hand these things over to Saint Joseph to do with them whatever he sees fit, Saint Joseph humbles himself and acts towards us as if he were a servant to attend to our needs! In this, he fulfills the words of Jesus: "He who is greatest among you shall be your servant" (Mt 23:11). In this, too, he is like his son Jesus, who came "not to be served but to serve" (Mk 10:43).

Clearly this text recommends consecration to Saint Joseph, since it reports all the blessings which follow upon such a consecration. Who would want to limit his blessings? Consecration to Saint Joseph amplifies our goods of body and soul, especially our interior life and our exterior deeds. Surely, the Lord will be generous to a soul who is not yet consecrated to Saint Joseph, but he will be even more generous, exceedingly more generous, to the soul who has consecrated himself to Joseph and Mary.

Theological Demonstration That Christians Should Consecrate Themselves to Saint Joseph

Now that we see this clear recommendation of consecration to Saint Joseph in the typological sense of Scripture, can we find a conclusive argument for the same conclusion in the New Testament? I think the answer is yes. Here is the argument in summary form: God wills that goods be returned to Him through the very same means by which He confers those goods upon us. And God has conferred upon us

His greatest gifts, the gifts of grace, through Saint Joseph. Therefore, God wills that we return those same gifts to Him through Saint Joseph. But consecration to Saint Joseph is nothing other than returning the gifts of God to Him through Saint Joseph. As a result, God wills us to consecrate ourselves to Saint Joseph. In this argument, there are two premises which need to be further investigated and established. The first premise is the general principle that God wills that goods be returned to Him by means of the same instruments through which He gives them to us.

This statement is verified throughout Scripture, and is especially true in regard to divinely established authority. For example, Saint Peter teaches: "Be subject for the Lord's sake to every human institution, whether it be to the emperor as supreme, or to governors as sent by him to punish those who do wrong and to praise those who do right. For it is God's will" (1 Pt 2:13–15). Saint Paul is even more explicit: "Let every person be subordinate to the higher authorities, for there is no authority except from God, and those that exist have been established by God. Therefore, whoever resists authority opposes what God has appointed, and those who resist will incur judgment" (Rom 13:1–2).

He further explains that it is a matter of having a blameless conscience that we pay taxes. So Saint Paul is obviously commanding that we return to God temporal goods we have received through the ministry of temporal authority through our respect and payment of taxes to those very same temporal authorities.[75]

---

[75] In this, Saint Paul echoes the words of Jesus "render unto Caesar the

When Jesus is being tried by Pontius Pilate, He does not deny that Pilate has some kind of authority over Him. Rather, He says, "You would have no power over me unless it had been given you from above" (Jn 19:11). This is striking that Jesus admits that as man, a man enrolled within the Roman Empire,[76] He is somehow subject to the authority of Pilate, precisely because His Father had established that authority!

This principle also extends beyond merely temporal authority. When describing the spiritual authority of His disciples, Jesus says, "Truly, truly, I say to you, he who receives any one whom I send receives me; and he who receives me receives him who sent me" (Jn 13:20); and again, "He who hears you hears me, and he who rejects you rejects me, and he who rejects me rejects him who sent me" (Lk 10:16). Notice that Jesus teaches that the return is to be made in the reverse order of the sending. The Father sends the Son, and the Son sends the apostles. So the return to the Father is first made through the apostles (by receiving them) and then through the Son (by receiving Him).[77]

---

things that are Caesar's." Surely, the coins of Caesar belong to God since to him belongs the world and all it holds. Nevertheless, since God has provided this money through Caesar, He expects us to return it to Him through Caesar by paying our taxes.

[76] Cf. Lk 2:1–5.

[77] Something similar happens in the Trinitarian missions: the Father sends the Son, and the Father and the Son send the Holy Spirit. As a consequence, we return to the Father in the Spirit and through the Son. We might further note that we find a kind of created likeness to this order of Trinitarian missions in the order among Jesus, Mary, and Joseph. Jesus communicates grace through Mary, and Jesus and Mary communicate this grace to us through Joseph. Consecration to Joseph then is simply an acknowledgment of the fact that our graces have been received from Joseph and ought to be returned through him as well.

In general, God wills that goods be returned to Him by means of the same instruments through which He gives them to us. This leads us to the second premise which needs to be investigated—namely, that God has conferred His greatest gifts, the gifts of grace, upon us through Saint Joseph. This statement has already been established in the foregoing chapters. Saint Joseph is the patron of the Universal Church, the provider of the Eucharist, the patron of a happy death, and so on. The foundation of all these truths is the clearly revealed truth that Saint Joseph cared for Mary and Jesus and, as a consequence, now has care of the Church which is the Mystical Body of Christ. Because his patronage is universal in scope, everyone has the duty to return these gifts to God through Saint Joseph by means of whom they were originally received. This makes Saint Joseph and Our Lady unique among the saints since their patronage is universal.

Making a Consecration to Saint Joseph

From these considerations, it is clear that consecration to Saint Joseph is something possible and is also according to God's will. To consecrate yourself to Saint Joseph, you simply entrust your entire self to Saint Joseph: your goods of body and soul, just as Jesus and Mary entrusted themselves entirely to his care. They allowed him to lead them to Bethlehem, then into Egypt, and then back to Nazareth, always trusting firmly in his care. A good consecration needs to be made deliberately and firmly, and so I recommend some time of prayer and preparation. Two excellent books for making a consecration to Saint Joseph are entitled *Consecration to Saint Joseph* by Father Donald Calloway and *Custos: Total Consecration Through Saint Joseph* by Devin Schadt. The latter consecration is for men only. Both books have a concluding prayer in which you make a voluntary offering of your life to Saint Joseph. There are many beautiful consecration prayers which can be used to make this consecration. I include the prayer written by Saint Alphonsus de Liguori for convenience, as well as another prayer which is modeled upon the Marian consecration prayer of Saint Louis de Montfort.

Consecration Prayer to Saint Joseph

Prayer by Saint Alphonsus

O Holy Patriarch, I rejoice with you at the exalted dignity by which you were deemed worthy to act as father to Jesus, to give Him orders and to be obeyed by Him whom heaven and earth obey.

O great saint, as you were served by God, I too wish to be taken into your service. I choose you, after Mary, to be my chief advocate and protector.

I promise to honor you every day by some special act of devotion and by placing myself under your daily protection.

By that sweet company which Jesus and Mary gave you in your lifetime, protect me all through life, so that I may never separate myself from my God by losing His grace.

My dear Saint Joseph, pray to Jesus for me. Certainly, He can never refuse you anything, as He obeyed all your orders while on earth. Tell Him to detach me from all creatures and from myself, to inflame me with His holy love, and then to do with me what He pleases.

By that assistance which Jesus and Mary gave you at death, I beg of you to protect me in a special way at the hour of my death, so that dying assisted by you, in the company of Jesus and Mary, I may go to thank you in paradise and, in your company, to praise my God for all eternity. Amen.

Another Prayer

Dear Saint Joseph, I (name) a faithless sinner, renew and ratify today in your hands the vows of my baptism. I renounce forever Satan, his pomps and works, and I give myself entirely to Jesus Christ, the Incarnate Wisdom, to carry my cross after Him all the days of my life, and to be more faithful to Him than I have ever been before.

I choose also to have as my mother and queen she to whom you were wholly devoted, Mary Immaculate. All that I have I offer to her, that I might be more perfectly conformed to Jesus, her Son. As you were consecrated to Jesus through her, so I also unite myself to Jesus through Mary, the Ever-Virgin Mother of God.

Finally, in order to be more perfectly consecrated to Jesus through Mary, and since you have found favor in my sight, I beseech you to attend to me, unworthy though I be, as Joseph of old once attended to the unworthy Egyptian. From this moment onward, I make you overseer of my house, of all my goods of body and soul, together with the value of all my good actions, and I place in your charge all that I have and am. I give you the full right to dispose of me as you will, since I am certain that your care for me will exceed any care I might have over myself. I hope in this manner to glorify God and to obtain His blessing upon all my interior and exterior acts, so that I might be ever more pleasing in His sight. I make this prayer through Christ our Lord. Amen.

Epilogue

What is there to say about a man who said nothing in Scripture? Much more than has been said in this little book. Only in heaven shall we see how much might have been said about the silent Saint Joseph. There are many other truths we might have investigated (for example, the many beautiful truths taught about Saint Joseph in his litany). But what Saint John of the Cross once said about Scripture might be also applied to Saint Joseph: the more we seek, the more we find. He is like a deep and inexhaustible mine where new treasures are found wherever we search. May devotion to Saint Joseph usher in a new age of the Church, an age in which the faithful rediscover and place themselves under the care of their spiritual father, Saint Joseph. May his glory shine ever more radiantly in heaven and on earth, and his devotion among the faithful flourish more lavishly.

Saint Joseph, pray for us!
October 7, 2021
Feast of the Most Holy Rosary

Appendix

Demonstrating the Existence of Purgatory

As posited earlier, Saint Joseph is the guardian and provider for the souls in purgatory. And yet, purgatory, like Saint Joseph's life, often remains a mystery if you don't look deep enough. As a result, many Christians, even Catholics, have doubts about purgatory since they believe Scripture is silent on the matter. Therefore, I have added this little appendix to lay out the basic argument for the existence of purgatory. This argument will be based upon truths clearly taught in Scripture.

To establish the existence of something, we must first say what the name means. For if we have no idea what the name means, we cannot assert if there is something in reality corresponding to the name or not. The name purgatory means *a temporary state after this life in which a human soul is punished for sins done in its life.*

Scripture unambiguously teaches (1) that the human soul exists after separation from the body as a distinct individual; and (2) that the deliberate actions of individuals deserve either reward or punishment; and (3) that in this life the goods and evils that people receive are not always proportionate to the rewards or punishments they deserve; and (4) that God is just and that He gives to each one as His deeds deserve; and, finally, (5) that not every sin deserves eternal punishment. These five premises form the basis of the argument for the existence of purgatory. Let us see the evidence for each premise.

Premise 1: The Human Soul Exists After Separation from the Body

Luke 16:22–23 says: "The rich man also died and was buried; and in Hades, being in torment, he lifted up his eyes, and saw Abraham far off and Lazarus in his bosom." Luke 12:4–5 declares: "I tell you, my friends, do not fear those who kill the body, and after that have no more that they can do. But I will warn you whom to fear: fear him who, after he has killed, has power to cast into hell; yes, I tell you, fear him!" Mark 12:26–27 says: "And as for the dead being raised, have you not read in the book of Moses, in the passage about the bush, how God said to him, 'I am the God of Abraham, and the God of Isaac, and the God of Jacob'? He is not God of the dead, but of the living; you are quite wrong." All of these texts clearly assert the existence of a living being after death.

Premise 2: Deliberate Actions of Individuals Deserve Either Reward or Punishment

In Matthew 16:27, Jesus says, "For the Son of man is to come with his angels in the glory of his Father, and then he will repay every man for what he has done." Saint Paul writes in Romans 2:5–8, "But by your hard and impenitent heart you are storing up wrath for yourself on the day of wrath when God's righteous judgment will be revealed. For he will render to every man according to his works: to those who by patience in well-doing seek for glory and honor and immortality, he will give eternal life; but for those who are factious and do not obey the truth, but obey wickedness, there will be wrath and fury." Revelation 14:13 states, "I heard a voice from heaven saying, 'Write this: Blessed are the dead who die in the Lord henceforth.' 'Blessed indeed,' says the Spirit, 'that they may rest from their labors, for their deeds follow them!'" Finally, it says in Ecclesiastes 3:17, "God will judge the righteous and the wicked, for he has appointed a time for every matter, and for every work."

Premise 3: In This Life the Goods and Evils That People Receive Are Not Always Proportionate to the Rewards or Punishments They Deserve

The entire book of Job is simply a response to this fact. Job is innocent and yet suffers terribly. Even more remarkable is the case of Our Lord and His mother, Mary, both of whom had no sin, yet suffered more than anyone else. On the other hand, we see those who are evil prospering: Psalm 73:3–5 says, "For I was envious of the arrogant, when I saw the prosperity of the wicked. For they have no pangs; their bodies are sound and sleek. They are not in trouble as other men are; they are not stricken like other men." Finally, in this life, the rich man who neglected Lazarus lived in complete prosperity (see Lk 16).

Premise 4: God Is Just and Gives to Each What They Deserve

Hebrews 6:10 states, "God is not so unjust as to overlook your work and the love which you showed for his sake in serving the saints." Saint Paul says in 2 Thessalonians 1:6 that "God deems it just to repay with affliction those who afflict you." In 2 Corinthians 5:10, Saint Paul also says, "For we must all appear before the judgment seat of Christ; so that each one may receive good or evil, according to what he has done in the body."

Premise 5: Not Every Sin Deserves Eternal Punishment

In 1 John 5:16–17, it says, "If any one sees his brother committing what is not a mortal sin, he will ask, and God will give him life for those whose sin is not mortal. There is sin which is mortal; I do not say that one is to pray for that. All wrongdoing is sin, but there is a sin which is not mortal." Jesus says in Luke 12:47–48 that "the servant who knew his master's will, but did not make ready or act according to his will, shall receive a severe beating. But he who did not know, and did what deserved a beating, shall receive a light beating. Every one to whom much is given, of him will much be required; and of him to whom men commit much they will demand the more." Finally, Proverbs 24:16 says, "A righteous man falls seven times."

Now that we have evidence for each of these premises, we can put them together:

If the soul exists after separation from the body (premise 1) and deserves reward or punishment (premise 2), then if God is just (premise 4), it must either be rewarded or punished in this life or the next. But it is clear that it is not always justly rewarded or punished in this life (premise 3). Therefore, it must be rewarded or punished in the next life. The punishments of the next life could be explained by hell if the only punishment which people deserve when they die is eternal separation from God. But it is clear that not all the punishments of the next life deserve hell (premise 5). Therefore, there must be punishments in the next life which do not eternally separate us from God (i.e., temporary punishments). But recall that the name purgatory means a temporary state after this life in which a human soul is punished for sins done in its life. Hence, we have proved that purgatory actually exists.

Scripture confirms this conclusion more directly. According to Saint Matthew's Gospel, Jesus states the following: "Make friends quickly with your accuser, while you are going with him to court, lest your accuser hand you over to the judge, and the judge to the guard, and you be put in prison; truly, I say to you, you will never get out till you have paid the last penny" (Mt 5:25–26).

No one gets out of hell, so Jesus must be talking about purgatory.

Again, Saint Paul says:

> By the grace God has given me, I laid a foundation as a wise builder, and someone else is building on it. But each one should build with care. For no one can

> lay any foundation other than the one already laid, which is Jesus Christ. If anyone builds on this foundation using gold, silver, costly stones, wood, hay or straw, their work will be shown for what it is, because the Day will bring it to light. It will be revealed with fire, and the fire will test the quality of each person's work. If what has been built survives, the builder will receive a reward. If it is burned up, the builder will suffer loss but yet will be saved—even though only as one escaping through the flames. (1 Cor 3:12–15 Vulgate)

What does it mean to "suffer loss" and escape through "flames" on the "Day"? It can't mean hell, since such a one "will be saved." Saint Paul was clearly talking about purgatory.

Jesus also says in Matthew 12:31–32, "Therefore I tell you, every sin and blasphemy will be forgiven men, but the blasphemy against the Spirit will not be forgiven. And whoever says a word against the Son of man will be forgiven; but whoever speaks against the Holy Spirit will not be forgiven, either in this age or in the age to come." This implies that some sins are forgiven "in the age to come." But no sins are forgiven for those in hell. Therefore, Jesus must be referring to purgatory.

And this is exactly what is asserted in the Second Book of Maccabees:

> And they turned to prayer, beseeching that the sin which had been committed might be wholly blotted out. And the noble Judas exhorted the people to keep themselves free from sin, for they had seen with their

> own eyes what had happened because of the sin of those who had fallen. He also took up a collection, man by man, to the amount of two thousand drachmas of silver, and sent it to Jerusalem to provide for a sin offering. In doing this he acted very well and honorably, taking account of the resurrection. For if he were not expecting that those who had fallen would rise again, it would have been superfluous and foolish to pray for the dead. But if he was looking to the splendid reward that is laid up for those who fall asleep in godliness, it was a holy and pious thought. Therefore he made atonement for the dead, that they might be delivered from their sin. (2 Mc 12:42–46)

Finally, in the book of Exodus, the chosen people's journey corresponds to our individual spiritual journey. Saint Paul describes this connection in First Corinthians, where he declares, "For I do not want you to be unaware, brethren, that our fathers were all under the cloud and all passed through the sea; and all were baptized into Moses in the cloud and in the sea; and all ate the same spiritual food." Their bondage in Egypt under Pharaoh was an image of our bondage in sin under the devil. The ten plagues of Moses correspond to the way our sins are restrained by the Ten Commandments of Moses. Their passing through the Red Sea and the death of Pharaoh's troops correspond to Baptism and the destruction of the forces of the devil. Their being fed by the manna in the desert corresponds to our being fed by the Eucharist in this life. Their entrance in the Promised Land corresponds to our entrance into heaven. So what does the forty years of wandering in the desert correspond to? The Israelites wandered in the desert because they were not worthy to enter the Promised Land. So God sent them to wander the desert for forty years until they were ready (all those who were unworthy died off). The number forty in Scripture always refers to a time of cleansing or purgation (for example, there were the forty days of the flood, when the earth was purged of evildoers; many saints performed forty days of fasting as a purification to see God, etc.). So the forty years in the desert correspond to the time of purgation of a soul after death (when they reach the border of the Promised Land) and before heaven, when they enter into the Promised Land.

In conclusion, there is ample evidence for the existence of purgatory in God's word. To deny the existence of purgatory means to deny the truths revealed in Scripture.